WOLF MANKOWITZ
THE PLAYS

Wolf Mankowitz

THE PLAYS

THE SAMSON RIDDLE

•

THE HEBREW LESSON

•

THE BESPOKE OVERCOAT

•

IT SHOULD HAPPEN TO A DOG

•

THE MIGHTY HUNTER

OBERON BOOKS
LONDON

The Samson Riddle and *Essay* first published by Valentine, Mitchell, 1972
The Hebrew Lesson first published by Evans Plays, 1976
The Bespoke Overcoat first published by Samuel French Ltd, 1953
It Should Happen to a Dog and The Mighty Hunter first published
by Evans Plays, 1956

First published in this collection in 2006
by Oberon Books Ltd
521 Caledonian Road, London N7 9RH
Tel: 020 7607 3637 / Fax: 020 7607 3629
e-mail: info@oberonbooks.com
www.oberonbooks.com

A catalogue record for this book is available from the British Library.

ISBN: 1 84002 699 5 / 978-1-84002-699-3

Cover collage *Picture* © Wolf Mankowitz 1989

Printed in Great Britain by Antony Rowe Ltd, Chippenham

Contents

Preface

BY ANTHONY DUNN

Wolf Mankowitz was born in 1924 in Whitechapel, East London, to immigrant parents of Russian-Jewish stock. He attended East Ham Grammar School and was the first boy to win an Exhibition scholarship to Cambridge, where he studied English under F R Leavis, married Ann Seligmann, a fellow-student at Newnham College, co-edited the university's literary journal *Sheaf*, and, after war-service in the mines and the Royal Army Corps, was awarded his BA in 1946 and his MA in 1950. In the immediate post-war period he lectured extensively for the Workers' Educational Association, co-edited with Raymond Williams and Clifford Collins the influential left-literary magazines *The Critic* and *Politics and Letters*, began his journalistic career with *Time and Tide* and the *Sunday Pictorial*, and opened, with his sister and brother-in-law, an antiques shop in Piccadilly specializing in Wedgwood china. Mankowitz's scholarly interest in Wedgwood resulted in an important critical work, *The Portland Vase and the Wedgwood Copies* (1952), and his first novel, *Make Me An Offer* (also 1952), where an antiques dealer pursues a Wedgwood copy of the Portland Vase.

Mankowitz was an important and imposing figure in the literary and cultural life of 1950s and 1960s London. He enhanced his reputation as a novelist with such satirical works as *Laugh Till You Cry* (1955) and *My Old Man's a Dustman* (1956), wrote the screenplays for his own *The Bespoke Overcoat* (which won six awards, including Best Short-Story Film at the Venice Film Festival in 1955 and an Oscar for Best Two-Reel Short Subject in 1957) and *Expresso Bongo* (1959), as well as for *The Millionairess* (1960), *The Long and the Short and the Tall* (1961), *The Day the Earth Caught Fire* (1961), *Waltz of the Toreadors* (1962), and, with others, *Casino Royale* (1967); wrote extensively for *Punch*, *The Spectator* and the *Evening Standard*, and co-owned a restaurant, the Pickwick Club in Great Newport Street, a fashionable venue for a new generation of actors and producers such as Michael

Caine and Harry Salzman. But work took its toll, and in 1971, beset by health and financial worries, he moved to Ireland. He continued to write and teach, mostly as an adjunct professor of English and Theatre Arts at the University of New Mexico, as well as scripting films, notably *The Hireling* which won a Grand Prix at Cannes in 1973, and a televised series *Dickens of London* (1976). Prose works such as *Gioconda* (1987), *The Magic Cabinet of Professor Smucker* (1988) and *A Night with Casanova* (1991) explore the cultural significance of the 'trickster' figure, while *Exquisite Cadaver* (1990) and an exhibition of his collages in Dublin in the same year signal his late interest in Surrealism. He died in County Cork in 1998.

The five plays collected here dramatize what another Jewish novelist, Philip Roth, called 'the human stain'. Purities – of friendship, heroism, good intentions and, above all, language and texts – are smudged and begrimed by human desires and inadequacies. Jonah (*It Should Happen to a Dog*) is a travelling salesman landed with the role of doomsayer to the King of Nineveh; Morry (*The Bespoke Overcoat*) couldn't lower the price of a new overcoat for his friend Fender, whose death from the cold he has on his conscience; Samson is the hero of the Israelites against the Philistines but he has a weakness for women and finishes as an impotent icon in Gaza; Nimrod (*The Mighty Hunter*) conquers the world with the magical hunting suit Adam gives him, but his intentions for world peace are overcome by his pride in military achievement. Nimrod finishes babbling in back-slang what could be the Brecht-like watchword for all these plays: 'Remember you are only a man'. And Man has devised many languages, none of them pure, none of them The Word. Hebrew and Yiddish intermingle with English and Gaelic in *The Hebrew Lesson* to produce, not the Tower of Babel, but some common ground for understanding between the Rabbi and the IRA gunman. The Black and Tans stick rigidly to their own narrow, vulgar speech. Mankowitz levers open the sacred universalism of the Biblical narrative of Samson in three ways: by highlighting the different economic bases of the Israelites (agrarian) and the Philistines (commercial); by inventing a Philistine priest, Zoab, who suggests an anthropological explanation for the origin of

Jahveh; and by proposing a most unexpected figure as the real author of the Biblical story. Language, man's greatest invention, turns out to be the greatest impurity of all.

Wolf Mankowitz's witty and iconoclastic interrogations of his Jewish heritage can be read as part of a larger attempt to redefine, in the aftermath of 'The People's War', what 'the people' could mean in a time of consumer peace. His contemporaries Raymond Williams and Richard Hoggart attempted to answer the same question in their seminal works *Culture and Society* (1958) and *The Uses of Literacy* (1957). But these plays' greatest value today surely lies in their insistent scepticism towards any religio-political mania and their insistence on the primacy of the human imagination.

Anthony Dunn is Visiting Principal Lecturer in English at Portsmouth University and Wolf Mankowitz's official literary biographer.

THE SAMSON RIDDLE

This is the end of the matter;
all hath been heard:
fear God, and keep his commandments;
for this is the while duty of man.

ECCLESIASTES

The Essay

My father has, all his life, had an irresistible compulsion to accumulate books. Unlike most book-collectors, he then proceeds to read them with total concentration from beginning to end, as if searching for the secret of the world, which he knows must have been written down at some time, by someone. Always the book which could never exhaust his enquiring spirit has been the Old Testament; from him, I suppose, I acquired very early the habit of quite unreligious biblical study. I travel a great deal and have lived in many countries and the only book I ever carry with me is the Bible (in the highly readable edition of Ernest Sutherland Bates*). I have pondered and searched *Ecclesiastes* 'on the shores of Asia and in the Edgware Road', and have always found in it the answer to (or at least an attitude towards) my current perplexity, but *Samson,* however often I read it, has always left me with one or another riddle.

I began writing *The Samson Riddle* in Jerusalem, continued it in Rome and London, and finished it four years later in Dublin – a lot of places and too much time for a fast-moving professional writer to spend on any piece. When it was finished I found that what had escaped my normally commercially committed pen was not so much a play as an enquiry in dialogue form, with a Samson who does not suffer from giantism but is a normal reasonably well-made man at twenty, and a little gone to fat at forty. For I found nothing in the original story to suggest that Samson had ever been anything but ordinary physically. He had simply been chosen by God for a special task and so, when the need arose, he was loaned special powers. The mighty strength was a divine investment: it was not dependent upon muscle development. Samson's contemporaries and the public since have been mass-hypnotized by his reputation as they were (and are) by any Emperor's new clothes.

---

* *The Bible Designed To Be Read As Literature,* edited and arranged by Ernest Sutherland Bates (William Heinemann).

By the general public Samson is only remembered as a huge grotesquely comic idiot resembling Victor Mature, being betrayed by a fatal woman somewhere between Hedy Lamarr and Mata Hari, and revengefully pushing plaster columns down at Cinecitta in a low budget American-Italian spectacular. And yet, especially for a middle-aged Jewish artist, Samson embodies a number of fundamental riddles, and it was these riddles which began, one very hot afternoon in the then ruined building called the Khan in Jerusalem, to obsess me.

There is a condition much thought about today and known unamiably as 'the male menopause' which is particularly critical in artists and other men committed to the grandiose delusion of Purpose. In the late thirties it tends uneasily to manifest itself, a combination of fatigue, disillusionment and hope for a new, violent, and finally clear revelation. It is a malaise which seeks its resolution in strange countries, women, addictions, and affiliations. Men in their forties, their destinies already deeply committed, struggle to comprehend, twist, turn and shatter their lives in the attempt to break shackles of iron or gold, only, like Samson, to bend their heads finally to the forbidden question, offer the secret answer to the implacable enemy, suffer the inevitable blindness with deep relief, and go into seclusion to learn patience and await a clearer vision. It seems a unique and highly significant experience at the time, but is, in fact, a common concomitant of the onset of middle age and is, as I say, unflatteringly named by psychiatric doctors who have among their drugs many which may or may not successfully deal with endogenous or reactive depression. However, even after taking a pill the writing remains. The Book of the Judges contains this extraordinarily conceived and amazingly written story of Samson. It has haunted the imaginations and perplexed the intellects of artists through several thousand years of changing treatments for the problems of the male menopause; male delusions have risen and fallen in ruins about it while the story, like all great fables of the floundering of the human spirit in the drift of destiny, remains undamaged and unaltered. And the riddles it offers remain as essentially unanswerable as that of the Sphinx, for the true problem is, of course, in the answer. 'What goes on four legs, two legs, three legs?' It is the answer 'Man' which is the riddle.

Now as to Samson, many questions, all of them fundamental, arise. And many answers, all of them riddles, are offered. He is born late of a long barren mother and committed pre-natally to strange taboos and an obscure purpose. He must drink no wine, nor must his hair be cut, and he will 'begin' to lead his people out of bondage. But the restrictions are those of an indulgent society, and the bondage is a soft one. Samson's tribe is imprisoned by an idyllic agricultural life in a fertile country, and may not work iron. The masters are an indulgent, sophisticated (perhaps) Cretan people who worship the fertile and the beautiful, intermarry with their bondsmen, come to their weddings, gamble and hunt with them, and forbid them to live in urban centres, which are, anyway, cursed with the pollution of Dagonish worship, sacred prostitution and beautiful idols. Not such a difficult bondage to live in, an affluent and permissive society which ought to be a bad place for producing violent revolutionary heroes. But Samson sees a gentile girl and decides, for no great reason other than that 'she pleaseth me well', to marry her. No one objects very violently, because marrying-out goes on all the time in gently assimilationist societies. And so Samson's first major transgression against the taboos and commitments of his birth occurs, and the grinding mill of his God swings heavily into inexorable action.

To consider *Samson* first for what it will always be, an echo of Jewish culture, history and myth. Here is an account of a man raised from birth as a Nazarite – that is to say, he is committed to the fulfilment of a particular vow, he must 'begin to deliver Israel out of the hands of the Philistines'. Till such a vow was accomplished the Nazarite wore his hair uncut, eschewed wine, was not allowed to approach a dead body and foreswore women. Samson keeps his hair long and does not drink wine, but he takes honey from the dead body of a lion, is close to the dead he killed, and has a weakness for women, and gentile women at that. Three are mentioned: the Woman of Timnath, daughter of a Philistine vintner; the Harlot of Gaza, one of those sacred prostitutes who made Philistine places of worship appalling to the anti-erotic, anti-idolatrist Jewish puritans. And Delilah, the

Woman of Sorek, desperate final passion of a middle-aged Judge, his unforgettable betrayer. So, Samson radically reneges against the Nazarite commitment. Yet struggle as he may to change the destiny to which he has been committed pre-natally, he cannot do so. He can affect the smoothness of its flow but the end designed by Samson's God will, one way or another, through one blunt instrument or another, through this or that mistake, by whatever meaningless events and obscure rituals, come to pass. Nothing happens against the will of God, and whether we understand it or not, find it loving or sensible or not, everything has a reason and the reason is beyond ours.

One night in New York I went to the midnight court of one of the last reigning Chassidic rabbis, to the Brooklyn school of the *Lubavitcher Rebbe,* to look for answers to some of the extra-ordinary riddles asked by the Samson story. Once you pass through the door of the Brooklyn *stebl* in the decaying ghetto, where the night is owned by the laughter of Negro militants and the morning wakes early to the praying of orthodox Jewish students, their hair and side-curls like Samson's, you enter the world of Isaac Bashevis Singer. In a nicotine-coloured room of books and fading photographs of sublime rabbinic ancestors the *Rebbe* interviews his followers throughout the night, judges their disagreements, solves their problems, gives guidance, and discusses the question of why Samson, a chronic defaulter, fulfilled his destiny. 'For Samson,' he explains, 'was no different, no stronger, no purer, no less wilful and no less blind than any other man. He was chosen to accomplish a divine purpose not for his heroic qualities but simply because he was chosen. Once chosen his human deviations could complicate the process but not change it. The Almighty leads – men must follow.' As the *Rebbe* talks my feeling grows that man is dispensable, that his species is largely wastage and his life has no meaning he can begin to understand. I say so, and the *Rebbe* explains that because this can happen man's best course is to follow, unquestioningly, the *Torah.* If he does so he will move with the Divine Purpose without ever having to ask or know what it is.

'As to wastage,' explains the *Rebbe,* 'one seed is fertilized and a hundred thousand are not lost but return into the system of which that solitary fertilization is a part.' I feel that the difference between seeds and men is that each one of us is cursed and blessed with self-awareness. No other species is self-conscious, has an image of itself, continuously seeks identity. We are unable to enjoy so easily being the contribution of a seed to the nitrogen cycle. 'We are not important in the way in which we feel we are important, and we are important in a way in which we feel unimportant,' answers the *Rebbe*.

I ask two more questions about Samson. 'Why did he, knowing from experience that Delilah would betray him, nevertheless give her the secret of his strength?' The *Rebbe* explains that Samson was not responding to his reason but to the irresistible compulsion of his destiny. 'How often, when we do something unreasonable, do we truly express ourselves?' he undeniably observes.

My final question: 'Why did Delilah, with the world in her arms, betray it for silver?' Answer: 'Because she was a woman.'

It is nearly morning. Outside the door of the *Rebbe's* study the students wait, whispering like parchment, to ask me when I leave what he said. I am a Jewish alien and yet the *Rebbe* spent so long talking to me. Did he tell me the secret of the world? 'We talked about Samson,' I explained, and they are disappointed. 'Are you in trouble with a gentile woman?' asks one. 'We were talking about Samson,' I reply and walk into the dirty early morning street, more clear in my mind than I have been for a long time and, still not knowing the answers, less troubled by the abiding riddles.

To Gaza then I came, a few days after the Six Day War, to make a film about the emergent Israeli identity, and it seemed that the process Samson initiated was still in progress. The problem now – to secure the 'freedom' which results from the Samsonian way of being led out of bondage.

In Israel I became a purposive Jew, a sort of self-made time bomb of the country which had resulted from the distant actions of the Judges. As Tel Aviv relaxed from the efforts of killing more Philistines in six days than they had in the twenty years before, I observed that the city was not exactly Nazarite in its disposition.

The spirit of Samson was in the *nahals,* the settlements of young soldier-farmers, in the army, and in the still ideologically pure minds of many of the leaders of the country. As world opinion, which had a few weeks before been poised on the edge of heartbroken sympathy for a small, gallant, about-to-be-liquidated country, veered sickly into reverse, and, under the pressures of Russian, Arab, Left-Wing and merely traditionally anti-Semitic forces, began to project a ludicrously untrue image of Israel as a kind of Prussian-Jewish mutation, an aggressive little Semitic nazi with insane imperialist ambitions, it seemed possible that the commitment to fight the Philistines might last for ever. And, if so, could every phase of the battle be won? Supposing some future confrontation brought in powers whose strength would require the direct intervention of *Jahveh* in order to assure Jewish victory – shouldn't the Jews prepare by reassuming ultra-orthodoxy? Weren't we required by our history to become a Nazarite people? In the event such a total conversion proved (as it always does) impossible, should we not expect the bloody consequences of a modern Samsonian syndrome – the continuous attrition of our own and the enemy's human and material resources? The Arabs announced at regular intervals that they were committed to *Jehad*; was the Jewish commitment also to an endless Holy War? In a country where we heard and used the word 'peace' a thousand times a day, was there never to be peace?

I searched through Israel for answers and found that the daily emergencies of life made it impossible to live there with doubt. The two basic Israeli responses were and had to be, 'There is no alternative' and 'Everything is possible, including the impossible'. At the Western Wall I put on *tefillin* and prayed to a pre-Christian God whose miracles were of a quality which might appal christianized Jews, but were the essence of our terrifying Jewish history. And so, in menaced Israel, my projects in shards about me, I felt a warlike kind of security – that which comes of thinking one knows the enemy and where he is. Back in London, the clamour of liberal, Christian, socialist, democratic voices sounded like the bedlam of a Philistine love-hate feast. I was born and raised in England but I knew finally that though

England had not entirely made me, I had done nothing to make Israel and therefore had no permanent place there.

I now seemed able to read some of the runic marks on the Samsonian enigma. Samson's destiny had driven him to the place and moment when the lever of his forgotten strength could prize an unforgettable cause for vengeance out of his enemies. The Six Day War was such a lever. Israel could have, in twenty years, become a busy comfortable Levantine power, exchanging trade and culture with her neighbours, and, no doubt, the assimilating process would have blunted the historic memory of the Jews. But Israel was destined to remain Jewish; surrounded by a sea of implacable enemies the Jewish discussion of definition might continue but no one could talk himself out of being a Jew. And whatever pressures were upon Israeli Jews would be responded to by Jews elsewhere. The Samsonian definitive process is painful, but it works, and, because it has and does, another question throws its giant shadow across us.

Let me try to formulate that question. If Jews may be comfortably assimilated into other societies and peoples, and if this assimilation can, at the human level, show a pleasant return in living, why act against it? What, indeed, is the point of Jews remaining Jews either by their own efforts or by those of their enemies? Why must Samson pursue his painful individuation? Is there an end to the Jahvistic task? If Samson 'begins' the process, is it implied that there will be an *end* to it?

The dynamics of territorial affirmation are familiar and similar in all animal species. Political and physical reasons for grouping into territorially defined nationalities are equally unexclusive. The birds, the bees, lions and men all do it, although only the last kill their own kind for it. The pursuit of territorial identity, the redemption of a particular land after a two-thousand-year absence, the re-creation of a national image and actuality, while being valuable, even essential to the political and social security of the Jews, cannot reasonably be considered to be the *end*. Jewish purpose, the sole reason why the Jews may have been *Chosen,* the primary Jewish contribution to the development of Man, are the ethics and aesthetics of the Mosaic Code. And that Code, as Jewish nomadic history triumphantly demonstrates, is perfectly portable. In order to exist, infuriatingly and challengingly Jewish Identity requires only commitment to the Decalogue. Given that commitment (even nominally), a disparate group of peoples of vastly varying and even contradictory supra-cultures can be fused into a national unit strong enough to create a country whenever the historical opportunity presents itself. The spark, then, lies not in the Land, but in the Law; it lies not in the world but in the Word. On that piece of Jewish Sinai rock, the churches of the West have been built. Without it there is no western civilization. And yet, even with it, how few moments of civilized behaviour have there been during the three thousand years through which that Code has been promoted and protested, till now the whole western world with Judaeo-Christian principles sways on the edge of total self-annihilation? In such circumstances, if Jews are still 'chosen', what, one asks, are they chosen for? The answer must lie in terms of that highly portable, easily remembered, rarely observed Code. If the centres of civilization are destroyed in one holocaust, if Jerusalem itself with the last vestiges of the Temple and the national identity of the Jewish Israelis are all wiped out, somewhere, somehow, nomadic Jewish wanderers far from the centres of destruction will preserve the Code, and when ten of them meet in the desert of glass the civilizing process will begin again. It is not a prospect or a pattern to please us or make us feel secure in the pursuit of our vanities. But then happy endings are what children give to stories. Life demands only continuity, and perhaps the only safe assumption we may make about God's Nature is that it has a more consistent instinct for Life than we have, for our limited preoccupation is with our own lives. We cannot be pleased with playing the part of discarded seeds. And so it must have seemed to the men of Samson's time too, meaningless, cruel, impossibly burdensome and endless.

So to the temptations of idolatry. To find relief from the labours of Samson in pursuit of the intentions of an obscure and non-human, divine destiny, men invent gods they can understand, with passions like their own but magnified, and pleasures which they themselves can enjoy. Wine, wealth, power, death and sexual passion are the raw material of idols throughout Man's history, so that, since they are all monuments to human narcissism, there is comfort, relief and pleasure in their worship. But there is profound disillusionment as well, and revulsion and self-hatred; for, being *of* Man the idol must fail him in exactly the same ways that he fails himself. Hence, the embargo 'Thou shalt have no other gods before Me' is a warning against the direly negative results of the worship by man of himself. Woman is equally fatal, whether she be worshipped as Earth Mother, or Female Principle, or Sacred Harlot, or Divine Madonna, or Heavenly Wife. Instead of elevating themselves to a parnassian playground, man and woman should work equally together in the Task; otherwise, they exploit, fight, and destroy one another; for to be used, even as a vehicle of worship, is to be made into an object, and all human beings, one way or another, sooner or later, revolt against such abuse. Thus Delilah resents being used by Samson as a vacation from his labours, a distractor of his strength from its unpleasurable purpose. She recognizes that his use of gentile women for uncommitted sexual relief is a denial of their reality as human beings. Consequently, she and they must all betray him, for their need to protest their own reality (which is a kind of love for God's creativity) must be greater than their 'love' for Samson. By such unconscious protest human beings fight whatever would deny the reality of their 'souls', their sense, that is, of their being subjects only to God. And when no other resistance is possible, they will simply lie down and quietly give up their ghosts.

Addiction is a kind of idol-worship, and it is to release himself from it that Samson is compelled to reveal his secret, thus helping Delilah to help him to freedom by betrayal. Does that seem obscure? It isn't if we accept the end of the Samson story as intended; I mean the end as it relates to the history of the Jewish People, not the beautifully plotted story-elements in the original, the growing of the hair in the period of incarceration, and the return, after his prayer for revenge for the loss of his eyes, of his heroic strength. I believe that somehow or other a lot of Philistine nobles and priests did die when Samson died. I can see an ancient temple collapsing as a feast is in progress on its roof. I can believe that a blind hero, with his confidence and strength suddenly returned, could dislodge an ancient keystone.

21

Since, however, Samson's heroic dismantling of the Temple of Dagon is the only element of his story that can be assumed to be known to everyone who recognizes his name, I decided to take the liberty of a Jewish artist to meddle with Jewish history.

In *The Samson Riddle* I postulate a situation in which the shorn and blinded Samson has become not only weak but impotent; I invent a Philistine priestly plot to assimilate the mythical virility of a defeated hero-god-leader into their people's strength, and win compensation for their losses. It may perhaps be argued against my variation that it removes the final decision for what happens from Samson, and that, in a heroic story, the hero must at least be the cause of the final victory or defeat. I made the variation not simply as an amusing and feasible fiction, but to show that whatever happened the end result would be the same. The recorders of history and those with perfect hindsight make sure of that, and the instincts of the people for the inevitable, and the unbreakable sense of purpose that mothers have for their sons. I know very well that even if my account was certified truth they would have insisted upon the perfectly plotted, satisfyingly savagely horrific and unforgettably apt original ending.

I salute the unknown writer of the original and apologize for the deviations of my dialogue and action from his. He, pure Jew that he was, would, I hope, forgive me, insofar as I believe, as he did, that the task which Samson, the Jew, the Artist, Man, is committed to is the witnessing of the Word as best he can. It is a lonely and frequently unhappy commitment: 'It is not thy duty to complete the task, but neither art thou free to desist from it.' We must do, to the extent of our ability, the work that comes to hand. Only then may we achieve the identity for which we are chosen, fulfilling ourselves, like Samson, in spite of our deviations. So it is for Artists and Jews and Men.

'Where there are no men, be a Man.'

W.M.

Characters

SAMSON'S MOTHER

MANOAH

SAMSON

VINTNER

BRIDE, the Vintner's daughter

1ST SUITOR / PHILISTINE NOBLE

2ND SUITOR

3RD SUITOR

WOMAN

SCRIBE

THREE ELDERS

RABBI

DELILAH

MAID

DAN

BARBER

GIRL

ZOAB

OLD PRIEST

1ST PRIEST

2ND PRIEST

Suitors, Lords of the Philistines, Three Girls,
Two Priests, Women and Musicians

The Samson Riddle was first produced on 19 March 1972 as a reading at the Gate Theatre, Dublin, as part of the Dublin Drama Festival, with the following cast:

SAMSON'S MOTHER, Miriam Karlin
MANOAH, Hilton Edwards
DELILAH / BRIDE, Susannah York
SAMSON, Hugh Millais
VINTNER / BARBER / SCRIBE, Noel Purcell
RABBI, Liam Miller
ZOAB, Alun Owen

PRODUCTION NOTE

The Samson Riddle is designed to be produced on the barest possible stage with the minimum essential props and within three principal acting areas, between which movement is paralleled by cross-fading lights.

The costumes should be simple kaftans, white, black or striped, in silk or linen, depending upon the status of the characters.

The set should be a system of simple blocks and platforms at various levels, which are used as seats, tables, steps, etc, as required.

The music should be sparsely used and of an electronic nature, so as to build up to a large sound effect in the penultimate scene to simulate the destruction of the temple, during which special lighting effects are required.

The dialogue-style is deliberately eclectic and utilizes Yiddish rhythms, but should be played naturally without any strong over-accentuation of any kind. In the passages printed in bold type (which are quotations from the original story) the vatic effect should be momentarily underscored by lighting and a single musical chord, the lines being delivered at a slower pace and in a classical key.

It is not necessary to have a large cast. Apart from the principals, the cameos and trios of Suitors, Elders and Priests may be doubled as convenient.

Act One

SCENE ONE: MANOAH'S HOUSE

(*SAMSON'S MOTHER, a dignified, early middle-aged woman, is praying before a hermaphroditic effigy.*)

MOTHER: (*Intensively.*) You came to me, Angel, when I worked in the fields and you said, 'Behold thou art barren but thou shalt conceive and bear a son.' And where is he now Angel? We both know where he is. It's not my fault. I did as you told me. 'Drink not wine nor strong drink and eat not any unclean thing while you are pregnant,' you said, 'and you shall bear a son.' And I did, and I did. 'And no razor shall touch his hair, for the child shall be a Nazarite unto God from the womb.' I did it. Didn't I do it? And where is he now? Where is my Nazarite son? 'And he shall begin to deliver Israel out of the hand of the Philistines,' you promised. That little boy with long curls will begin to deliver us. And now he is a man with hair of gold and red, like rays of the sun, and where is that man, the hero of his people, that Nazarite pure from the womb? (*She suddenly bursts out, unable to contain herself.*) Whoring with the filthy bitches of Timnath, that's where he is! Damn all lying promises from men and angels!

(*She lashes out at the effigy, which falls to the stone floor and breaks. After a shocked moment she starts to pick up the pieces.*)

I'm sorry. I'm sorry. I didn't mean it. You can't know a mother's feelings. Excuse me, forgive me, Angel.

(*The latter part of her prayer has been observed by her husband, MANOAH, who has entered quietly and watched her, shaking his head deprecatingly. Now he joins her and on his hands and knees starts to help her pick up the broken pieces of the effigy.*)

MANOAH: (*Gently.*) Why do you talk to these idols, woman? You talk to them, you beg them, you scream at them, you shout at them, you kiss them, you break them. Figures of clay. What for?

MOTHER: I don't need any help from you.

MANOAH: But what is the sense of it, woman?

MOTHER: Sense? What's the sense of any of it?

MANOAH: (*Sighs.*) How can we know the sense of the Lord?

MOTHER: And that's you, isn't it? That's just how you are. No questions, just grovel and let it happen. Get up off your knees if you're a man.

MANOAH: I'm helping you, aren't I?

MOTHER: I don't need your help. Where's the head? Have you got the head?

(*MANOAH gets up and drops onto the floor the pieces of the idol he holds.*)

MANOAH: Clay, shaped by a potter in Gaza to something that is neither man nor woman.

MOTHER: (*Defiantly.*) My angel. (*Protectively, she picks up the pieces he has thrown down, then sighs as she studies them.*) This is too badly gone to repair. Never mind. (*She drops the pieces onto the floor, and gets up.*) I'll get another one. Maybe the blacksmith can make one in copper. Then it won't break.

MANOAH: So you'll have a copper angel, you can make copper prayers to it. What's to eat?

MOTHER: There's honey-cake and milk on the table.

MANOAH: So I'll eat. Shearing the sheep is hard work. The wool is thin this year. The price won't be so good.

(*He sits down and eats and drinks. The MOTHER has picked up a broom and sweeps up the broken fragments of the idol.*)

MOTHER: Sheep, wool, prices, eat. What about Samson? Where is he?

MANOAH: You, I and the angel know where he is. He's in Timnath.

MOTHER: And you eat – you drink – you shear the sheep.

MANOAH: (*Mildly.*) And you worship an idol.

MOTHER: That's different. Are you comparing me with those Philistine whores?

MANOAH: (*Still mild.*) Come woman – they're not all whores. The girl Samson goes to see is a fifteen-year-old virgin.

MOTHER: Any one of their fifteen-year-old virgins can become a sacred prostitute any time of the day or night.

MANOAH: All right, but her father's wine is the best in
Timnath and, furthermore, we have a treaty of friendship
with his people.

MOTHER: Friendship! We are slaves! We are conquered! They
do with us what they please.

MANOAH: So what do they do? They conquered our tribe
twenty years ago and since that time there has been no
war. We live in peace, they live in peace, our boys marry
their girls, their nobles marry our women. The only thing
is they won't let us work from iron. So what! Better they
should keep their secret weapons. For me a wood plough is
still good enough.

MOTHER: (*Defiantly.*) Why shouldn't we work from iron? With
iron we would destroy them.

MANOAH: That's why. Look – it all makes for peace. The
flocks grow. We worship in our way, they worship in their
way. The ways even get a little bit mixed up – as you
yourself know.

MOTHER: I know what I know. Don't you tell me what I
know.

MANOAH: (*Shrugs.*) All right. I'll finish my breakfast and get
back to the sheep.

MOTHER: That you can do but what will you do about
Samson?

MANOAH: (*With slight anger for the first time.*) What will I do?
I'll tell you what. What you've always permitted me to
do about Samson. Nothing. He's a child of prophecy, you
always told me. He's watched over by an angel, you said.
He has to be brought up this way and that way. He has
to have that ridiculous long hair. These are all your ideas,
woman. I spoke to the rabbi* about it, you know what he
said?

MOTHER: I don't care what he said.

MANOAH: I'll tell you. He said, 'What can I say? Samson is
a typical product of a permissive upbringing. Stubborn,

---

* There were, of course, no rabbis in the time of Samson. One of several
anachronisms produced by the Yiddish flavour of Manoah and Samson's
Mother.

wayward, wilful, tricky, strong-headed, wrong-headed, and certain to come to a bad end.' That's what the rabbi thinks. And me? I've got sheep to shear. (*He gets up and picks up his shears.*)

MOTHER: (*Appealingly.*) But Manoah, tell me.

MANOAH: (*Irritably.*) What? What?

MOTHER: What are we going to do about Samson?

MANOAH: He's coming now. Ask him yourself.

MOTHER: Don't you dare go. You stay. You face out something for once in your life.

MANOAH: There's still more than half the flock to shear.

MOTHER: You'll stay or I'll never speak to you again.

(*For a moment MANOAH considers the possibility, as if it wouldn't be so terrible if she didn't. Then he shrugs and sighs.*)

MANOAH: So I'll stay. (*He puts down his shears resignedly.*)

(*SAMSON enters. While being well-built, he is in no way a giant or strongman. His strength comes from God not from muscles. He is in his twenties, his hair red-gold in long wild ringlets. He carries over his shoulder the skin of a lion, fresh and bloody, which he throws down on the floor.*)

SAMSON: (*Uncertainly.*) Father and mother. Uh – good morning, isn't it?

MOTHER: (*With forced calm.*) So it's a beautiful morning. Good. Where have you been all night?

SAMSON: I brought you a lion's skin to keep you warm this winter.

(*MANOAH goes over to the skin and examines it.*)

MOTHER: Rugs we've got. Rugs we're not short of.

MANOAH: It is! It's another enormous mountain lion. You killed it yourself?

SAMSON: With my bare hands.

MANOAH: You see, woman? This is marvellous for the sheep-raising. Samson has killed so many mountain lions with his bare hands, we hardly lose a lamb any more. And you know what the percentage of losses to mountain lions used to be?

MOTHER: Don't bother me with economics. (*To SAMSON.*) Where were you all night?

SAMSON: What? I'm starving. What's to eat?
(*He drains a beaker of milk on the table and starts to eat honey-cake voraciously.*)

MANOAH: (*Admiringly.*) With his bare hands. How he does it on such a diet, I cannot understand.

MOTHER: You? You could never understand. Like everyone else your mind is too simple. But I believe. I know that if God wills it a midget can make a nonsense from a giant. My Samson doesn't have to be a monster to have a monstrous strength. He was an underweight baby and already I knew. He just has to live clean and be a good Jew. Samson, you're deaf all of a sudden? I asked where were you all night.

SAMSON: (*Mouth full.*) Where? In Timnath, where else?

MOTHER: All night?

SAMSON: (*Swallowing.*) Why not? We went hunting this morning. I made a bet with the Philistines.

MOTHER: So – gambling!

MANOAH: There's nothing that says a Nazarite boy can't gamble, woman.

MOTHER: And drinking perhaps you were?

SAMSON: You know I don't drink. I let them drink. That way the next day they won't hunt so well. (*He laughs.*)
(*MANOAH also laughs.*)

MANOAH: He's no fool, our boy.

MOTHER: And women? What about women?

MANOAH: What do you mean, what about women? He's a strong, normal Jewish boy. What do you want?

MOTHER: Were there women, Samson?

SAMSON: Certainly there were women.

MOTHER: (*Triumphantly.*) Philistine women!

SAMSON: A few Jewish women too. You know, wives of some of the Philistines.

MANOAH: Yes, that's another thing. This very Timnath girl's mother is Jewish.

MOTHER: (*Coldly.*) I was not aware that we were discussing a particular Timnath girl. Are we discussing something in

29

particular, because if so, as Samson's mother, I think I am entitled to know.

(*MANOAH and SAMSON exchange a glance.*)

MANOAH: (*Resignedly.*) You'd better tell her, Samson.

SAMSON: (*Evasively.*) Tell her? Tell her what?

MANOAH: With mountain lions a hero, but with his own mother – all right, I'll tell her. Samson wants to marry the Timnath girl.

(*The MOTHER is dumbstruck for a moment. Then she puts her hands to her head and covers her eyes.*)

MOTHER: No, never. It's not possible. They can't do this to me, they wouldn't.

(*SAMSON looks at her with bleak helplessness for a moment, then:*)

SAMSON: I'll help you with the sheep, father.

MANOAH: Good idea.

SAMSON: Let's go.

(*Their threatened exit brings the MOTHER together rapidly.*)

MOTHER: Where do you think you're going?

MANOAH: Samson's helping me finish the sheep.

MOTHER: Not until I've had my say, he's not.

MANOAH: But the sun is reaching its height. Who can shear sheep in the heat of the day?

MOTHER: Let the sheep drop dead. You listen to me.

(*To SAMSON.*)

Is there never a woman among the daughters of thy brethren or among all thy people that thou must take a wife of the uncircumsized Philistines?*

SAMSON: (*Coldly.*)

Get her for me; for she pleaseth me well.

(*There is a moment of silence as the MOTHER takes in the absolute finality of SAMSON's decision.*)

MOTHER: (*Brokenly.*) That's all you have to say to me, my son?

SAMSON: That's all. (*To MANOAH.*) Let us to work, father.

---

* Whenever the actual Biblical language is used a special tone of destiny enters the scene. The characters are for the moment possessed, and such quotations are played, as it were, in parenthesis to the body of the piece.

MANOAH: The wool is thin this year.

SAMSON: The drought last winter.

MANOAH: Water – that's the whole problem of this damned country, with water it would flow with milk and honey – (*They exit. The MOTHER stands agonized for a moment and then she drops to her knees.*)

MOTHER: (*Praying.*) A man came unto me and his countenance was like the countenance of an Angel of God – very terrible. And he said unto me… 'Behold thou shalt conceive and bear a son, and he shall be a Nazarite to God from the womb to the day of his death and he shall begin to deliver Israel out of the hand of the Philistines.'

SCENE TWO: AT THE FOLDS

(*Some time later; SAMSON and MANOAH have finished the sheep-shearing.*)

SAMSON: That's the last one. You're right, the wool is thin this year.

MANOAH: The drought is the curse of this damned country. My God, Samson, we finished the whole flock and it's still daylight. That strength of yours is no joke, my boy.

SAMSON: I wanted to finish early.

MANOAH: Uh-huh?

SAMSON: I told her father you would meet with him today.

MANOAH: You're really serious about marrying the girl?

SAMSON: I am.

MANOAH: But Samson – why marry? We could pay her father concubine money instead of bride money. You get your way, you send her back when you're tired of her, all it does is increase her value as a bride, your mother won't be upset, and there's no harm done to anyone. Why marry the girl Samson? (*SAMSON doesn't answer.*) I mean – what's so special about a fifteen-year-old Philistine girl?

SAMSON: She has thirty important Philistine suitors.

MANOAH: So she's a beautiful girl. When you've finished with her the suitors can bid for her. Why marry?

SAMSON: (*Uneasily.*) I know, I know. She giggles and wants to dance all the time yet I must marry her.

31

MANOAH: Look, Samson – we've all been in love a dozen times. There's nothing about love that marriage can't cure. But it's so drastic, son.

SAMSON: I must, that's all.

MANOAH: This is a very unnatural feeling for a young man. Can you describe it a little more?

SAMSON: To tell you the truth, father, the Voice tells me.

MANOAH: (*Dismayed.*) Oh no! Not that Voice again. You promised me you didn't hear the Voice any more.

SAMSON: Well, it's true – I don't hear it as often as I used to. But sometimes it still speaks.

MANOAH: Look, it makes no sense, my son. I can understand it when the Voice was saying to you as a small boy 'Guard the law', 'Build yourself up for the struggle against the enemy', 'Lead a clean life' and all that sort of stuff. This is what holy voices are supposed to say to a young fellow. But 'Marry a fifteen-year-old Philistine girl who giggles and dances' – is that something for a holy voice to say to a carefully brought-up Jewish boy?

SAMSON: What can I do? That's the message.

MANOAH: Listen, Samson – I know from my talks with the rabbi that the human mind is a very strange business. You're sure you're reading the message properly?

SAMSON: Father, there's no argument about this. The message comes through in pure Biblical Hebrew.

MANOAH: (*Sighs.*) Well, it's just another mystery, that's all. A holy voice sends you a ridiculous message in a language which hasn't even been fully invented yet.

SAMSON: I know it has something to do with my career. This marriage will affect my whole future.

MANOAH: You're damned right it will. For a boy as promising as you – to whom so many of the younger Jews look up with respect, a lot of them even saying they are going to vote you the next Judge – this decision can be a calamity. It's a terrible political mistake, Samson. Do me a favour. Let's offer her father double the concubine price and forget the marriage.

(*SAMSON stands as if listening to something. His father looks at him hopefully. Then SAMSON shakes his head and sighs.*)

SAMSON: Sorry, father. The message is quite clear. I have to marry the girl.

MANOAH: You have to marry her, eh?

SAMSON: (*Resignedly.*) I have to. But somehow I don't think it's going to be a straightforward, normal marriage like you and mother.

MANOAH: Please God. All right then. Let's go and make the deal. As a matter of fact, with the wool so poor this year, even the bride price I am going to have to argue about a little bit.

SAMSON: The girl and her father are mad for me. She won't be expensive.

MANOAH: Well, that's a blessing anyway. We'd better go. It's a fair walk to Timnath.

SAMSON: On the way I'll show you the carcass of the mountain lion I killed.

MANOAH: I'd like to see it. You know killing all these mountain lions has got you a wonderful reputation. (*He sighs.*) It's a pity you have to lose it for a giggling girl with St Vitus dance. Still, that's how we men are when it comes to girls.

SAMSON: I told you, it's not the girl – it's the Voice.

MANOAH: All right, it's the Voice, it's the Voice. But I still say that's how we men are when it comes to girls.

SCENE THREE: THE HOUSE OF THE TIMNATH VINTNER

(*PHILISTINE SUITORS, dressed identically in white silk robes, sit around at the end of the feast to celebrate SAMSON's marriage to the VINTNER's daughter.*

SAMSON and MANOAH sit to either side of the VINTNER. In a separate area are the WOMEN of the VINTNER's family around the WOMAN OF TIMNATH, a fifteen-year-old girl dressed in bridal clothes. Her face is veiled.

The VINTNER is a typically affable, heavily built, middle-aged merchant farmer – very Jewish – with a strong accent.)

VINTNER: Drink, drink, my friends. Enjoy, enjoy. This is – I
    say it without false modesty – the best wine of the best
    vineyard in all our beautiful country of Philistia, including
    the occupied territories of our dear friends and neighbours
    with whom today we pledge yet another bond of friendship
    and peace. To you thirty noble, distinguished, handsome
    suitors who have complimented my house by paying your
    addresses to my beautiful daughter, I say thank you from
    the bottom of my heart. I only wish that I had what it takes
    to give you a daughter apiece. But at my age, even on
    my wine, not even the Harlot of Gaza herself can do very
    much for me. Mind you – I still have my moments – don't
    I, Mothers? I get no complaints from my seven wives. But
    gentlemen, enough is enough and I am sorry that with
    the best will in the world, I cannot satisfy you all. I mean
    you thirty distinguished suitors – not you seven happy,
    happy wives. So here we are together, friends. My old
    friend Manoah – a great fellow, even if he is a Jew – and
    my marvellous, fantastic, heroic new son-in-law, Samson.
    I cannot tell you what it means to a father when one of his
    seventeen favourite daughters makes such a marriage. Also
    friends, do not let us overlook the political significance of
    the occasion. By marrying this beautiful girl of mine…
BRIDE: (*Giggling.*) Oh, Daddy, stop…
VINTNER: …Samson forges a bond of association between
    our two peoples which, we all know, from twenty years
    of happy living together we do not really need. But on
    the other hand – it doesn't do any harm to know that an
    instrument like Samson is on our side. So now, before the
    happy couple retire…to check over their wedding presents,
    let me thank my old friend Manoah for the marvellous
    gift of two pedigree rams. One is already looking after
    my ewes, and the other… (*He indicates SAMSON.*) …soon
    will be. (*Laughter.*) Let me also thank Samson himself for
    bringing as a present some of the best honey I have ever
    tasted. I did not know that you were a great bee-man as
    well as a great sheep-man, Manoah, but that honey, that
    was something special. And now I am going to stop boring

you all with the ramblings of a happy father and ask my distinguished son-in-law Samson to say to you a few words before he disappears for the ritual seven days with my lovely daughter whom I give to him with the deep feeling in my heart that, if I may coin a phrase, I am not losing a daughter but gaining a champion for our people.

(*SAMSON stands up. There is an expectant silence as he looks around and seems unable to find anything to say.*)

MANOAH: (*Whispers loudly.*) Say something, Samson. This is an occasion.

VINTNER: (*To MANOAH.*) The boy is overwhelmed, no?

MANOAH: (*Urgently to SAMSON.*) Samson, speak. Speak!

(*SAMSON makes noises, but no clear words emerge from his mouth.*)

1ST SUITOR: Look at him! He's so dumb!

BRIDE: With a body like that who needs to talk?

MANOAH: (*Loud whisper.*) Please Samson, something, anything. (*Embarrassed to VINTNER.*) The boy is over-whelmed, you understand. You have made such a marvellous occasion here. We are a simple people. The lad's not used to it.

VINTNER: (*Put out.*) I understand. But something he should say.

SAMSON: (*Declaims suddenly.*)

Out of the eater came forth meat, And out of the strong came forth sweetness.

(*There is silence for a moment and then puzzlement.*)

VINTNER: (*To MANOAH.*) What did he say?

MANOAH: (*Hurriedly.*) It's a riddle, friend. Among our people great occasions are commemorated with magical riddles.

VINTNER: Oy! What a people! (*To SAMSON.*) All right, son-in-law – it's a riddle, friends. Say again, Samson.

SAMSON: **Out of the eater came forth meat, And out of the strong came forth sweetness.**

VINTNER: Beautiful. But what does it mean?

MANOAH: (*Quickly.*) You see, it means like if you are strong you can also be a very sweet person. No, Samson?

SAMSON: (*Quietly.*)

If ye can certainly declare the answer to me within the seven days of the feast, then I will give to you thirty Philistines thirty sheets and thirty changes of garments. But if ye cannot declare it to me then shall ye give me thirty sheets and thirty changes of garments.

VINTNER: (*Delighted.*) I understand! What a boy! What a gambler! He knows our people love a gamble. What do you say, lads? Do you accept the bet of my brilliant son-in-law?

SUITORS: Why not? We'll gamble on anything! It's easy. What was it? Out of the strong came forth meat. No, no… (*Etc.*)

VINTNER: Very good, Samson. My thirty noble friends will answer your riddle. (*Aside to MANOAH.*) If they can, which frankly I don't believe, because what sense does it make?

MANOAH: (*Aside.*) The sense that it makes, dear friend, is that Samson is going to bring to your beautiful daughter a marvellous trousseau.

VINTNER: He's a clever boy.

MANOAH: (*Proudly.*) Not clever, friend, inspired.

VINTNER: Hup! Let the dancing begin.

(*A small group of Philistine MUSICIANS starts to tune up. The BRIDE leaps to her feet.*)

BRIDE: Mother of Dagon, I thought they'd never finish. (*She calls to the SUITORS.*) I'm going to dance with all of you for the last time. Who's first?

1ST SUITOR: As the first of all your suitors, bride, I claim the right of the first dance.

2ND SUITOR: Since when was there any such right?

1ST SUITOR: Since now. (*He draws his dagger.*)

BRIDE: (*Petulantly.*) No fighting on my wedding day. I won't dance with anyone who kills anyone.

(*The MUSICIANS break into a jerky Philistine number.*)
(*To 1ST SUITOR.*) Come on then. (*As they dance.*) I love this song. It's the rage of Gaza.
(*As they DANce the BRIDE and the 1ST SUITOR are isolated from the party.*)

I suppose you often go to the Temple of Gaza?

1ST SUITOR: My family are hereditary oil-bearers.

BRIDE: I've never been.

1ST SUITOR: You never will, now.

BRIDE: I will if I want to.

1ST SUITOR: A good Jewish wife in the Temple of Dagon
– please!

BRIDE: I can go into any temple I want.

1ST SUITOR: That's what you think.

BRIDE: I can and I will.

1ST SUITOR: You just don't know what being a Jewish wife
means.

BRIDE: I do so. My mother's Jewish.

1ST SUITOR: Not for the Jews she isn't any more.

BRIDE: She always goes when Daddy visits the sacred
prostitute. She loves it.

1ST SUITOR: But do you ever see the wives of any Jews there?

BRIDE: What difference does that make?

1ST SUITOR: You'll find out.

BRIDE: You're just jealous.

1ST SUITOR: Of that big idiot?

BRIDE: If he's such an idiot, answer his riddle.

1ST SUITOR: I will.

BRIDE: So give me the answer.

1ST SUITOR: No, baby bride. You give me the answer.

BRIDE: (*Puzzled.*) What do you mean?

1ST SUITOR: (*After a beat, and in a sinister tone.*)
**Entice thy husband that he may declare unto us the
riddle.**

BRIDE: Why should I?

1ST SUITOR: **Entice him lest we burn thee and thy
father's house with fire.**

BRIDE: You wouldn't dare.

1ST SUITOR: We would, baby bride, we would.

BRIDE: (*Shocked.*) Burn me and my father's house?

1ST SUITOR: With fire. (*The music dies away. The BRIDE stares at
the 1ST SUITOR, frightened.*)

BRIDE: (*Quietly.*) **I will entice him.**

SCENE FOUR: THE MARRIAGE CHAMBER

(*The BRIDE drifts from the dancing area, leaving the 1ST SUITOR behind her. The lights reveal SAMSON waiting, combing his hair thoughtfully. She starts to undress.*
As she takes off her veil she looks towards him expectantly. He ignores her.)

BRIDE: I've taken off my veil.

SAMSON: Oh yes.

BRIDE: My veil.

SAMSON: Yes.

BRIDE: It's off.

SAMSON: Yes.

(*The BRIDE bursts into tears.*)

BRIDE: I've never been so insulted in my life.

SAMSON: What's the matter?

BRIDE: You didn't dance with me.

SAMSON: I don't dance. You danced with everybody else. What are you crying about?

BRIDE: (*Wails.*) You're my husband and you don't even want to look at me the first time I take off my veil!

SAMSON: Of course I want to look at you. Come here.

BRIDE: No.

SAMSON: Please come to me.

BRIDE: I don't want to.

SAMSON: I want to see your face.

BRIDE: No you don't.

SAMSON: I do.

BRIDE: I don't know why you married me if you don't want to look at my face.

SAMSON: I tell you I do.

BRIDE: Then why didn't you look at me when I took off my veil? There's thirty noble Philistine suitors would knife one another to death for such a sight. (*She starts to sob again.*) And you just go on combing your ridiculous hair.

SAMSON: Look, my dear –

BRIDE: (*With sudden realization.*) Oh Mother of Dagon! No! –

SAMSON: (*Puzzled.*) What?

BRIDE: You're a pederast!

SAMSON: I? (*He laughs.*) Ask them in Gaza!

BRIDE: Oh, they were right when they said 'Have fun in the vineyards with them, but never, never marry one. They're all perverts.' They were right!

SAMSON: Look, you dirty minded little whore –

BRIDE: 'Oh no,' I said, 'I've known a few of those Jewish boys and there's nothing like that about them,' I said. More fool me! Oh woe is me – woe – nothing but woe!
(*She sinks down onto a bed of sheepskins.*)
Thou dost hate me and lovest me not.

SAMSON: Look, let's get a few things clear. I don't hate you, and I am not one of your Philistine temple sodomites. It's just that I've a lot on my mind at present.

BRIDE: (*Sobs.*) Oh woe is me – woe – nothing but woe.
(*SAMSON kneels down beside her on the bed and tries to comfort her.*)

SAMSON: Come now. This is our wedding night. Will you cry it away?
(*The BRIDE pulls away from him like a wildcat.*)

BRIDE: Don't you touch me. You long-haired thing – you big, stupid Jew.

SAMSON: (*Discomfited by the girl's venom.*) Look here – even a Philistine woman is supposed to respect her husband.

BRIDE: Why should I respect a man who doesn't love me?

SAMSON: I do. I do.

BRIDE: Don't lie to me.

SAMSON: Why would I marry you if I didn't love you?

BRIDE: Some filthy Jewish plot, I suppose. Oh you're so cunning your lot!

SAMSON: A marriage couch is not the place for an anti-Semitic demonstration. Is it?

BRIDE: Look at him. Big, strong, beautiful and absolutely useless to a woman.

SAMSON: (*Annoyed.*) You fork-tongued little Philistine bitch!
(*He smashes her across the face with the back of his hand. She collapses onto the bed. The BRIDE looks up at him, a new light dawning in her eyes.*)

BRIDE: You do love me!

SAMSON: Love? Love is the talk of girls and the action of men.

BRIDE: But –

SAMSON: (*Brutally.*) Shut your mouth and open your legs.

BRIDE: (*Meekly.*) Yes, husband.

SCENE FIVE: THE TENT OF THE SUITORS

(*Three of the SUITORS are sitting huddled together gambling with dice in a desultory sort of way as they discuss Samson's riddle.*)

2ND SUITOR: Out of the eater came forth sweetness.

3RD SUITOR: Meat, meat, you fool.

2ND SUITOR: Meat, I mean. And out of the strong came forth weakness.

3RD SUITOR: Sweetness, you idiot, sweetness.

2ND SUITOR: All right, sweetness. Can somebody please tell me why we are sitting around like a bunch of bloody rabbis arguing the ins and outs of some stupid Jewish conundrum?

3RD SUITOR: Because if we don't work it out it's going to cost us a lot of silk, that's why.

2ND SUITOR: So – out of the strong came forth meat. What does that mean?

3RD SUITOR: From the strong came forth the sweetness, imbecile.

2ND SUITOR: Oh yeah. It's from the eater came forth the meat.

3RD SUITOR: I think I've got the answer. Out of the eater came forth meat. Right?

2ND SUITOR: Right.

3RD SUITOR: So that means the eater who eats meat is himself for somebody else, meat. Right?

2ND SUITOR: Oh – great solution I'm sure, like steaks eat steaks. Where does that get us?

3RD SUITOR: And out of the strong came forth sweetness. Well, that's got to mean something that's strong can also be like – very nice.

2ND SUITOR: Oh please. I mean, let's smoke or drink or some thing. This is just wasting the whole night.

3RD SUITOR: So we enjoy ourselves and it'll cost us a fortune. Is that clever?

2ND SUITOR: No, look – why not? I mean there's a lot of very strong things that if you tame them you can keep them around the place. Like a fox. I knew a fellow had a tame fox –

3RD SUITOR: What's so strong about a fox?

2ND SUITOR: All right then – a bull is strong. But a bull can be very, very sweet. My uncle has a bull. He's just like one of the family.

3RD SUITOR: (*Laughs.*) The Vintner has a bull and he *is* one of the family.

(*The 1ST SUITOR, who has been listening to all this, now speaks.*)

1ST SUITOR: Relax, gentlemen. I have the solution.

2ND SUITOR: So tell us, tell us.

1ST SUITOR: When I know, you shall know.

2ND SUITOR: What does that mean?

3RD SUITOR: That means that like the rest of us, he doesn't know.

1ST SUITOR: Not yet – but I will – and you will – and that arrogant circus-strongman will lose this game.

2ND SUITOR: I don't know what we're all getting so concerned about anyway. I mean, a silk robe and a bed-sheet – I've lost more than that on a turn of the dice before. It's not such a big deal – and we had a marvellous dinner.

3RD SUITOR: Listen, it's not the price – it's the principle.

1ST SUITOR: Exactly. If we allow these Jews to ridicule us there will be no end to their effrontery.

2ND SUITOR: Oh come on – they're nice people. We've lived with them a long time now. We never have any trouble.

1ST SUITOR: You forget that before we conquered them they raided our territories, captured our women, burnt our temples, ridiculed our gods. Don't be fooled by this peace and quiet between our peoples. Give them an inch, they'll take a yard. Give them a yard, they'll take a mile. Give them ten miles and they'll take Gaza itself.

3RD SUITOR: (*Uncomfortably.*) I don't like this kind of talk. I'd rather lose the bet. What the hell. Anyone for dice?

1ST SUITOR: That's right, gentlemen. Play on. Relax. Enjoy yourselves. We've won.

2ND SUITOR: (*Rolling dice.*) I'm glad you think so. All right. Here they roll. Come on, babies, show daddy three beautiful phallic symbols. Huh!

(*The game continues.*)

SCENE SIX: THE MARRIAGE CHAMBER

(*SAMSON lies on the couch staring at the ceiling.*
The BRIDE is curled up, turned away from him, huddled under
a sheepskin.)

SAMSON: What was that?

(*The BRIDE throws the sheepskins off her head.*)

BRIDE: I said, that was some marriage night.

SAMSON: We'll improve. You move around like a snake.

BRIDE: That's how they taught me at the temple. Our priestesses know more about this kind of thing than your old fogies will ever know.

SAMSON: Why make such a big thing of it?

BRIDE: (*Indignantly.*) Why? I'll tell you why? Because I'm supposed to have a climax, that's why. What do you think the other girls in my clan would say if they knew on my marriage night I didn't have a climax?

SAMSON: You know too much about sex. It's not healthy.

BRIDE: You are, I suppose.

SAMSON: I haven't had any complaints before from your women.

BRIDE: Of course you didn't. Our girls are too polite, that's why. Also with us it's a religious duty before marriage. We're not looking for pleasure. But after marriage – what the hell else is there in it for us? Babies?

SAMSON: For a fifteen-year-old girl your ideas are deplorable.

BRIDE: I'm a wife, and a wife can say what she likes. Furthermore, she is entitled to a climax.

SAMSON: Let's forget it now. I'm tired.

(*The BRIDE jumps up from the bed, absolutely furious.*)

42

BRIDE: You're tired! What do you think you've done? Killed a thousand mountain lions or something? I mean – really – if that tires you I can see I'm in for a marvellous married life.

SAMSON: Can't you understand? I've had a lot on my mind the past few days.

BRIDE: Maybe it's on your mind, big man, but it certainly isn't anywhere else.

SAMSON: I have special problems.

BRIDE: You can say that again.

SAMSON: Anyway, I understood from your father that you were an innocent, sweet little virgin.

BRIDE: So?

SAMSON: So where's the evidence?

BRIDE: (*With great dignity.*) I am a certified technical virgin.

SAMSON: What's that?

BRIDE: It means that since the age of twelve I have only consorted with men on a purely religious basis. And I have a certificate to prove it.

SAMSON: So you're not a virgin.

BRIDE: I'm a virgin to marriage, aren't I? And so far as I'm concerned, even after marriage I'm still a virgin.

SAMSON: (*Indignantly.*) But you've been with other men – God knows how many.

BRIDE: (*Coolly.*) I know exactly how many. How could I pass my exams if I didn't know exactly how many? Oh, it's a waste of time talking to you. You're just an ignorant Jewish shepherd brute. You know nothing about the refinements of life.

SAMSON: And you do, of course.

BRIDE: I graduated second in my class for Courtship Technique, third for Deviations and first in Massage, Cretan style.

SAMSON So?

BRIDE: So what? (*Suddenly distracted.*) Your latissima dorsi are huge.

SAMSON: Teach me something.

BRIDE: (*Weakening.*) I'm not going to teach you anything until I'm sure you love me. Why should I?

SAMSON: I love you. I must love you.

BRIDE: No.

SAMSON: I'm insane with love for you. I hear voices.

BRIDE: I don't believe you.

SAMSON: Look, how can I prove I love you?

BRIDE: Well, you failed the first test – miserably.

SAMSON: Forget it, please. I was worried. And also the place is unfamiliar.

BRIDE: (*Sagely.*) That's true. In sexual congress unfamiliar circumstances are a prime source of anxiety. That's one of our lessons. Maybe you do have a little excuse.

SAMSON: You see?

BRIDE: But only a little one. I still don't know yet that you love me.

SAMSON: So how do I prove it?

BRIDE: If a lover tells his beloved a secret known only to himself, this is considered conclusive proof of love and will create a climate congenial to successful connection.

SAMSON: (*Shrugs.*) All right – but what secret can I tell you?
(*The BRIDE now approaches SAMSON very seductively, and twines herself around him like a slim little serpent. She looks up into his eyes, kisses his face, descending to his lips, and then after a long lingering embrace which leaves him rocking, speaks:*)

BRIDE: **Thou hast put forth a riddle unto the children of my people and hast not told it me.**

SAMSON: **Behold, I have not told it my father nor my mother, and shall I tell it thee?**
(*The BRIDE withdraws from him.*)

BRIDE: There – you see – you don't love me. You impotent, stupid, sexless, unloving Jewish brute.

SAMSON: (*Hurriedly.*) All right then. I'll tell you the answer to the riddle.
(*The BRIDE approaches him again and puts her arms about him.*)

BRIDE: (*Whispers.*) My lovely, virile, gorgeous, enormous, sweet and loving Jewish brute. Tell me, tell me!

SCENE SEVEN: THE TENT OF THE SUITORS

(*The THREE SUITORS stand waiting as SAMSON approaches.*)

1ST SUITOR: **What is sweeter than honey? And what is stronger than a lion?**

(*SAMSON stops amazed.*)

SAMSON: What did you say?

1ST SUITOR: 'What is sweeter than honey? And what is stronger than a lion?' What do *you* say?

SAMSON: (*After a pause.*)

I say that if ye had not ploughed with my heifer, ye had not found out my riddle.

(*The 1ST SUITOR smiles and the other SUITORS look at one another with smiles of satisfaction.*)

1ST SUITOR: When will you pay, friend?

(*SAMSON suppresses his tremendous anger.*)

SAMSON: When I collect, friend.

1ST SUITOR: When shall we know, friend?

SAMSON: Friend – you will know.

(*The SUITORS start to disperse. The 2ND SUITOR starts to speak to SAMSON.*)

2ND SUITOR: Look, Samson, women are neither Jewish nor Philistine but a separate nationality, why fall out over them? (*SAMSON stares at him.*) Oh, never mind!

(*He exits after the others. SAMSON stands for a few moments. his head bent as if listening. He shakes his head as if to clear it and hear better. MANOAH enters and watches him.*)

SAMSON: (*Aside.*) I do not hear you clearly. No. I do not hear. Your voice is lost in the roar of the fountain of fire which burns in my blood.

MANOAH: Why so much anger for so small a cause? The girl is kin to them. They threatened her. Frightened, she spoke. It's an expensive joke, Samson, that's all.

SAMSON: Whose joke?

MANOAH: Your joke – your riddle – these tricks go against oneself sometimes. It's the luck of the game.

SAMSON: Whose game?

MANOAH: The game, the game we play to pass the time and keep the mind from worse things. Thirty lengths of silk cost maybe a flock and a half of sheep, but it's not the end of the world. Come.

SAMSON: But this game – this joke – this trick which starts with an engagement in Timnath, proceeds to an encounter with a lion, continues with a nest of bees, forms itself into a riddle and discovers in its answer betrayal and fury – whose joke is this?

MANOAH: Forget it. Tonight we'll sleep. Tomorrow I'll ask the rabbi. Why do you hesitate? What do you hear?

(*SAMSON is listening attentively.*)

SAMSON: I must go to Ashkelon.

MANOAH: To Ashkelon? Why? In Ashkelon the Philistines are laughing tonight over your defeat. Why look for trouble? Better to pay up and forget it.

SAMSON: I go to Ashkelon – to pay.

MANOAH: And forget it?

SAMSON: The jokes of Jahveh are unforgettable. (*He exits.*)

MANOAH: Please, Samson… (*He sighs.*) I suppose he is my son, but every day I see less resemblance. (*Shaking his head sadly, MANOAH exits.*)

SCENE EIGHT: THE HOUSE OF THE TIMNATH VINTNER

(*The VINTNER is in a high state of excited anxiety. He paces back and forth, shouting.*)

VINTNER: Bring wine. Has she come back yet?

WOMAN: She'll be back soon.

VINTNER: I never heard of such a thing. Such a barbarian! Such a peasant animal I should welcome into my house! Oh Dagon, forgive me for my heart is too big, my nature too generous, my mind too unquestioning. What can they do to me for this?

WOMAN: What can they do to you? It's not your concern.

VINTNER: He's kin, isn't he? This bloody monster is our kin! Oh the shame of it! The danger of it! Where is that idiot girl? There aren't enough noble suitors of our own people for her taste. She has to have a Jewish monster to bring trouble on my house. (*He shouts.*) Where is she?

WOMAN: She's coming. She's coming.

VINTNER: She can't even go and get me the scribe without making a whole argument out of it. (*Falsetto.*) 'I'm a married woman now. I don't have to run errands.' (*Reverts to normal voice.*) What a marriage! What a calamity!

WOMAN: What an excitement! Maybe it's not even true.

VINTNER: Not true! In Ashkelon I saw the robes myself. Crimson they were with the blood of his victims, thirty fine Philistine boys, boys from Ashkelon. In a great pile he threw their robes down, steaming with blood, before the thirty noble suitors. 'Now I have paid,' he said. Thirty fine young men of our people lose their lives, so that he may make his bloody jokes. My God – I must find out my legal position. Where is that slut of a daughter of mine?

WOMAN: She's here. She's here. With the Scribe.

(*The BRIDE enters with an elderly Philistine SCRIBE.*)

WOMAN: (*To BRIDE.*) What took you so long?

BRIDE: You expect me to run like a child? I'm a married woman.

VINTNER: You married woman, get out! (*He slaps her hard across the backside and she exits noisily.*)

WOMAN: It's not the girl's fault.

VINTNER: (*Screams.*) Get out, all of you. Damned stupid women! Where's the wine?

WOMAN: It's there, it's there. (*She indicates the table, and exits.*)

VINTNER: (*To SCRIBE.*) Take some wine. (*The SCRIBE goes to take wine.*) No, don't. We haven't got time. You heard?

SCRIBE: Your son-in-law is proclaimed throughout the country as the murderer of thirty fine young men in Ashkelon. He's a strong boy. I'm so out of breath. I'll take a little. (*He pours himself a little wine.*)

VINTNER: So you heard – so tell me.

SCRIBE: It's a beautiful wine.

VINTNER: I sent for a lawyer, not a drinking companion. (*He snatches the goblet away from the SCRIBE.*) What is my legal position?

SCRIBE: Well – he *is* kin.

VINTNER: Thank you. This I know. To be told this I don't have to pay a scribe a barrel of good wine every year.

SCRIBE: On the other hand. Supposing the marriage was never consummated –

VINTNER: (*Indignantly.*) What do you mean, never consummated? You think I would give my favourite daughter to an impotent?

SCRIBE: We all know it was consummated – but if it hadn't been, then in our law it would be no marriage.

VINTNER: (*Getting the point.*) It was never consummated. My daughter will swear it.

SCRIBE: In such a case the woman would be eligible for another husband, and then from a purely legal point of view I don't see how you could be considered the kin of Samson.

VINTNER: Me, the kin of that alien devil? The very suggestion is an insult. Draw up a marriage contract immediately.

SCRIBE: With whom?

VINTNER: With one of the thirty good, honest Philistine suitors.

SCRIBE: All right. But which one?

VINTNER: Questions, questions. Pick any suitor.

SCRIBE: And the bride price?

VINTNER: Forget it. In this case, I'm paying.

(*SAMSON enters from behind the VINTNER. The SCRIBE sees him.*)

Why are you standing like you've been struck dumb?

(*SAMSON advances into the eyeline of the VINTNER. His clothes are bloodied.*)

(*Nervously.*) Oh Samson, I'm glad to see you. (*To SCRIBE.*) Go now and do as we have agreed.

SCRIBE: I go, I go. (*He hurries out.*)

SAMSON: I would go in to my wife.

VINTNER: But –

SAMSON: What?

VINTNER: Look, I thought you hated her, so I gave her to one of our own boys. But look, Samson, I'll give your father back the whole bride price, plus a flock of first-class ewes. And I'll stand the loss of the wedding, which didn't cost buttons. Fair, Samson?

SAMSON: (*Sighs deeply.*)
Now shall I be more blameless than the Philistines.
(*He turns to go.*)
VINTNER: Samson –
SAMSON: (*With savage coldness.*) Yes, Philistine.
VINTNER: (*Pleading.*) What will you do now, Sir? You won't
do something ridiculous? After all –
SAMSON: What I must do, I will do.
(*The VINTNER collapses utterly.*)
VINTNER: Dagon, protect us poor ordinary people. What will
this raving lunatic and his insane God do next?

SCENE NINE: MANOAH'S HOUSE

(*It is night. A small lamp burns.*
MANOAH is at the table, eating. SAMSON'S MOTHER is serving
him.)
MOTHER: So where is Samson?
MANOAH: I told you before. He's catching foxes.
MOTHER: (*Angrily.*) Stop making ridiculous excuses. Where is
he?
MANOAH: He's catching foxes.
MOTHER: If you must lie for the boy, think of a clever lie.
MANOAH: (*Wearily.*) Look. For the past three days he didn't go
to the sheepfolds. I saw him this morning on the hill. I said
to him, 'Where have you been?' He said to me he's been
catching foxes.
MOTHER: My son the furrier! By you men, a woman is
expected to believe anything.
MANOAH: I'll take some more of the goat cheese.
MOTHER: You've had all there is. What will he do with the
foxes?
MANOAH: What will he do? How do I know what he will do?
The Philistines have two regiments of soldiers looking for
him and he is suddenly an animal lover! What do I know
about Samson?
MOTHER: He's really catching foxes?
MANOAH: He says he needs three hundred.
MOTHER: Why so many?

MANOAH: Why not? At least it's good for the flocks. The foxes take a lot of kids. You know – maybe after that unfortunate business in Ashkelon he feels he should atone with a little social service. That could be it.

(*During MANOAH's speech a flickering red light from flames in the fields outside starts to illuminate the room.*)

MOTHER: (*Worriedly.*) The boy is getting so I don't know him any more. That marriage was a terrible mistake. I always said so. The whole thing was a shock to his system. What's this light?

MANOAH: It was a shock to the whole social system. There are always incidents among the young but thirty Philistines killed in cold blood – it's not so easy to overlook.

(*The MOTHER crosses to the door.*)

MOTHER: What's all the light?

(*MANOAH now notices the increasing red light from the spreading fires in the countryside. He gets up startled.*)

MANOAH: What is it?

MOTHER: (*Alarmed.*) There's flames spreading everywhere! It's a fire!

(*The light from the flames increases. MANOAH stands beside her at the door looking out towards the back of the auditorium.*)

MANOAH: The flames are spreading like red quicksilver – here and there, low to the ground. I never saw such a fire before.

MOTHER: The sheep! Go to the folds!

MANOAH: The fire doesn't move that way. It moves towards Timnath.

MOTHER: But the wind blows in the opposite direction.

MANOAH: Yes. The fire moves against the wind! This I never saw before.

MOTHER: It's a miracle!

MANOAH: What are you talking about – a miracle? What good does a fire bring anyone? I'll go to the sheep.

(*He hurries out. She watches the fire fascinated.*)

MOTHER: (*Fervently.*) Fire of the Angel, burn the Philistines. Burn them. Burn them.

SCENE TEN: THE HOUSE OF THE TIMNATH VINTNER

(*The same flames are being watched by the terrified VINTNER and his family. But the flames are brighter and stronger from their angle.*)

VINTNER: (*Shouts.*) The flames are coming closer!

BRIDE: But the wind – the wind blows the other way.

WOMAN: The fire runs across the ground like snakes, like scorpions.

VINTNER: It flows across the ground. Look, look!

BRIDE: (*Terrified.*) I see animals of fire running through the corn.

WOMAN: No, the animals are not burning, but between them something burns.

BRIDE: Look, look – what is that great dark figure standing above them?

WOMAN: I see the light on his face.

BRIDE: It is him!

WOMAN: It's him! It's him!

BRIDE: (*Screams.*) It is Samson! I see his hair angry in the flame-light. I am afraid, father.

(*The 1ST SUITOR enters with his companions. The red light now burns fiercely.*)

VINTNER: What has the man done?

1ST SUITOR: **Three hundred foxes he has caught and took firebrands and turned tail to tail and put a firebrand in the midst between two tails. And when he had set the brands on fire, he let them go into our standing corn and burnt up both the shocks and also the corn with the vineyards and olives.**

VINTNER: (*Appalled.*) This has he done?

3RD SUITOR: Aye, this he has done because you took his wife and gave her to our companion.

VINTNER: (*To 1ST SUITOR.*) You are my kin now. Speak for us. What say you, son-in-law?

1ST SUITOR: I say burn them who have brought the fire to our people.

VINTNER: (*Eagerly.*) Aye, the Jews, the Jews. Burn them!

1ST SUITOR: And I say burn the friends of the Jews.

VINTNER: (*Eagerly.*) Aye, burn them. They are as bad and worse. Burn them!

1ST SUITOR: Let all Philistines remember the fire that Samson hath kindled.

VINTNER: (*Savagely.*) We shall remember!

1ST SUITOR: Let the vengeance of Dagon consume the enemies of our people.

VINTNER: Aye – let them be all consumed.

1ST SUITOR: And let the friends of our enemies burn with them.

VINTNER: Aye, let it be so!

(*The 1ST SUITOR indicates to his companions that they should set fire to the VINTNER's property. They start to do so. There are screams of terror from the WOMEN. The VINTNER throws himself upon the 1ST SUITOR.*)

What are you doing? Are you as mad as he?

1ST SUITOR: Only by a madness as great as his shall his madness be defeated. (*Shouts.*) Fire the vineyards! Fire the houses! Let not one child of this accursed clan escape!

SCENE ELEVEN: SAMSON'S CAMP AT ROCK ELAM

(*A cave in the mountain which SAMSON has made his head-quarters. MANOAH argues with him.*)

MANOAH: (*Wearily.*) Samson, Samson, this one-man war against a whole people is ridiculous. In the end you cannot win.

SAMSON: In the end our people will follow me and we shall win. I suppose.

MANOAH: You're not even sure?

SAMSON: The voice says what it has always said. I am to begin to free the people. Begin.

MANOAH: All right – say we win. What will we win? A devastated land, the crops all burned, the cattle dead, the sheep crying skeletons, the old men gibbering and every woman, Philistine or Jewish over the age of ten, raped by somebody or other. If it's racial purity you're working for, this also you won't get by war.

SAMSON: Father – I am not making war at the moment. I am not even planning it. All I am doing is hiding up here from the Philistines.

MANOAH: Of course. That's all you are doing. Except that if, by any chance, a few dozen Philistines are stupid enough to find you, you wipe them out.

SAMSON: That's purely self-defence. After the burning of the Timnite and his family, I stated categorically that I would smite the Philistines, 'hip and thigh with a great slaughter' – and that is a direct quote, whatever the enemy propagandists may say to the contrary – 'and after that I will cease'. That is what I said. And that is what I meant. Any conflict between us since that time has not been of my seeking.

MANOAH: After they burnt the Timnite you should have considered the whole business fairly settled and left it alone.

SAMSON: How could I see my father-in-law and wife murdered like that and not make some nominal protest?

MANOAH: You slaughtered all the Suitors, all their retainers and three platoons of crack police cavalry. Really, Samson – for a small country your ideas of slaughter are too big. Couldn't you have just made it the Suitors?

SAMSON: Look, father, I have already stated publicly that I consider the whole unfortunate incident closed.
(*MANOAH sighs deeply.*)

MANOAH: I have to tell you, my boy, that our Philistine neighbours don't feel the same way.

SAMSON: Rest for a while – take something to drink – it's a long hard climb up here.

MANOAH: Samson, I cannot rest – I cannot drink – I didn't only come to you as your father. I bring with me other reverend elders of our tribe and of the tribe of Judah.
(*THREE ELDERS enter, white bearded, wearing fringes. SAMSON stands up, suddenly excited.*)

SAMSON: Judah has rallied to me at last! Now shall I begin!

MANOAH: They have rallied all right.

SAMSON: With the forces of Judah and our own tribe the Philistines will be certainly defeated. (*He turns to the ELDERS.*) I thank you, Elders of Judah, for your support. Send your judges to me. Let us hold council together.

1ST ELDER: Three thousand men of Judah are rallied in the valley below, Samson.

SAMSON: Judah is a lion.

2ND ELDER: And beyond them are pitched the Philistines who have spread themselves in Lehi.

SAMSON: Then, father, go quickly back to our people and have them travel speedily through the night and meet up with the power of Judah.

MANOAH: Not so quickly, Samson. Listen, listen.

3RD ELDER: Samson, knowest thou not that the Philistines are rulers over us?

SAMSON: Now shall their rule be broken, Reverend Elder.

2ND ELDER: They are rulers over us, Samson. What is this that thou hast done unto them?

SAMSON: (*Puzzled.*) What is this you ask now? I challenged them – they cheated me – I revenged myself – they took vengeance upon the innocent – again and finally I answered them with great slaughter – and after that the matter should have rested so.

1ST ELDER: And now their great army is pitched in Judah and spread in Lehi.

SAMSON: But the men of Judah are three thousand and fearless.

1ST ELDER: The men of Judah honour their treaty with the Philistines.

SAMSON: (*Astounded.*) Why then do you come to me?

2ND ELDER: (*Embarrassed.*) This is what we ask the Philistines. 'Why are ye come up against us?' we ask.

3RD ELDER: And they answer: 'To bind up Samson are we come up. To do to him as he hath done to us.'

2ND ELDER: So we are come to bind thee that we may deliver thee into the hand of the Philistines.

(*SAMSON is dumbstruck by their submissiveness.*)

SAMSON: (*To MANOAH quietly.*) And you father, do you also come to deliver me to the enemy?

MANOAH: I come to you as a father, not as an Elder of our tribe.

SAMSON: And as a father, what do you tell me, father?

MANOAH: As a father I tell you to escape – escape and fight.

(*The ELDERS express their shock in murmurs.*)

SAMSON: And as an Elder of our tribe how do you speak?

MANOAH: (*Sighs.*) I say, weigh Samson in one scale and the people of Dan and Judah in the other and tell me which lies heaviest upon my heart.

(*SAMSON makes up his mind and stands up.*)

SAMSON: (*To ELDERS.*)

Swear unto me that our people will not fall upon me themselves, for I cannot defend myself against our people.

1ST ELDER: **We will bind thee fast and deliver thee into their hand; but surely we will not kill thee.**

(*He nods to the 2ND ELDER who produces two new cords from around his shoulder and comes forward.*)

SAMSON: You, father, shall bind me.

MANOAH: I?

SAMSON: (*Gently.*) You alone, father. You bind me, father.

(*MANOAH binds him expertly and silently. The others lead SAMSON off. MANOAH looks after him expressionlessly for a moment and then walks into the next scene.*)

SCENE TWELVE: MANOAH'S HOUSE

(*The MOTHER stands looking enquiringly towards MANOAH, who walks into the area.*)

MOTHER: So where is Samson?

MANOAH: With two new cords we bound him and brought him up from the rock.

MOTHER: (*Disgustedly.*) There are no men left in the world but him. And then?

MANOAH: And when he came unto Lehi the Philistines shouted against him.

MOTHER: Now he was bound, they could shout.

MANOAH: Will you tell the story or shall I ?

MOTHER: Tell, tell.

MANOAH: And the spirit of the Lord came mightily upon him.

MOTHER: (*Triumphantly.*) Of course.

MANOAH: And his bonds loosed from off his hands.

MOTHER: (*Eagerly.*) And then, and then?

MANOAH: And he found a new jawbone of an ass and put forth his hand and took it.

MOTHER: (*Ecstatically.*) My boy – my hero – my Samson.
(*Lighting up at back of them to reveal SAMSON standing, his clothes torn, his body streaked with blood, the blood-streaked jawbone hanging from his hand. We dim the lighting on MANOAH and SAMSON'S MOTHER in the foreground to hold them frozen. SAMSON looks with dull horror at the jawbone in his hand.*)

SAMSON: **With the jawbone of an ass, dead upon dead.**
(*Lighting comes up in the dark area around SAMSON to reveal group after group of Philistine dead. The lighting continues to come up until the entire area is revealed full of corpses in grotesque positions – a mute inferno of the slain.*)
With the jaw of an ass have I slain a thousand men.
(*Disgustedly he tosses the bone away. Lighting up on MOTHER and MANOAH.*)

MOTHER: And then, and then?

MANOAH: And then the men of Dan called him their judge and their captain. For this ass's bone has finally cloven our people away from the Philistines and from this time on there will be war.
(*The MOTHER is seeing it all with ecstatic eyes.*)

MOTHER: That's my son. I always knew he would win that election. Samson – my son, the judge.
(*Lights fade slowly.*
End of Act One.)

Act Two

SCENE ONE: SAMSON'S CAMP AT ROCK ELAM

(*SAMSON has been a Judge of Israel for twenty years. Now in his early forties, immensely powerful, but coarsened by the long years of guerilla warfare, he sits, moody and depressed, listening to a seemingly endless harangue from an old RABBI, who is accompanied by an ELDER and his father, MANOAH.*)

RABBI: To put it in a nutshell, Samson, the people are tired of war, and who can blame them? A war that drags on year after year for nearly twenty years is no longer just a war, Samson. It's a way of life. And it's a life for a dog. Every Spring the crops are planted, every Summer the crops are burned. The standard of living throughout the tribes has never been lower. The young men are all fighting with you in the hills, interested only in the bloody business of warriors, our birth rate has dropped to an all-time low, and the Philistines, who used to be such a nice, relaxed, civilized people, have become a rabble of bloodthirsty lunatics. Who can win such a war?

SAMSON: Wars are for fighting, Rabbi. Victory is an illusion resulting from a single successful battle. The war always continues.

RABBI: But to what end?

SAMSON: You, a rabbi, ask me about ends? I am an instrument of means, Rabbi. You are the expert on ends. Tell me the end.

RABBI: I do not know the end of the Lord.

SAMSON: To the Lord there is no end. But I tell you this, Elders of the Tribes, in the war men find themselves, and each other. They stand up, are counted, recognize their friends, confront their enemies and are identified.

ELDER: And dead!

SAMSON: Dead perhaps, but identifiable. Dead as themselves.

MANOAH: (*Gently.*) It's an answer, Samson. But is it a good enough answer? Our shepherds use their shears for cutting throats. Our ploughmen make billhooks from their ploughshares. Our farmers-boys leave the fields.

SAMSON: To defend them.

MANOAH: To fight the Philistines. This doesn't defend fields. This burns them.

SAMSON: Father, gentlemen, I suggest you return to your villages before curfew. Afterwards I cannot be responsible for your safety.

RABBI: At least hear our case.

SAMSON: Tell it in Gaza – tell it in Ashkelon – tell it to the Philistines. Are they not in arms against me?

RABBI: Philistine threats you don't have to take so seriously. You know how they blow hard. Show a little friendship, Samson, and even after twenty years of slaughter, maybe they will respond.

SAMSON: They are committed on the heads of their gods to eliminate us. To show friendship to your enemy is idiotic.

ELDER: (*Sighs.*) Aah! When we lived quietly among the Gentiles, we had peace. From time to time the wilder currents of their life swept us up. But in ourselves we had peace because we knew that it was not our business. We were the victims of their history. Our own went on quietly, secretly.

RABBI: Spiritually, he means. We were a subject people dispersed among the Gentiles, but spiritually we were one.

ELDER: We were born quietly.

RABBI: We lived quietly.

ELDER: We died with not much noise. Nothing to draw attention. Nothing to invite scorn, or envy, or fear of strangers.

RABBI: That was our spiritual unity, untouchable, beautiful and dedicated to the Lord.

ELDER: True we had transgressors. I hate to think of the mixed marriages. And the consumption of unclean foods increased all the time. I know. It was my job to check the butchers' shops.

MANOAH: There was even a certain amount of harmless idolatory. But basically the spirit of the people was sound.

RABBI: In fact, the spirit was sounder because we had
these tests to contend with. Because we were peacefully
surrounded by the Gentiles so we had the more to
concentrate upon those small differences which preserve
our peaceful identity.

SAMSON: And now you are Jews.

RABBI: We were Jews then – always.

SAMSON: Aye – Philistine Jews. Philistine citizens of the
Jewish persuasion.

RABBI: That's so bad?

MANOAH: It's not so unreasonable. The people think of the
old times and of the old ways and they long to return to
them, even if it means a little bit of slavery here and there.
After all, everything has its price.

SAMSON: And the cost of war to the enemy must be death.
So we kill them, without hatred, without pleasure, without
revenge.

MANOAH: What is there left to kill them with?

SAMSON: Reason – we kill them with sufficient reason.
(*The RABBI sighs deeply.*)

RABBI: So for Samson there is reason in all this – sufficient
reason.

ELDER: You're mad, Samson.

RABBI: Come, friends, there is no more to say.

ELDER: And soon for Samson's sake, no breath to say no
more.

RABBI: Aye – we shall die, we shall die.

SAMSON: Yes, old man, and my young men too. And I also,
most horribly will die.

RABBI: And in this end you see sufficient reason for the laying
waste of the peace and quiet of us and our enemies. What
is it by you, Samson? Is it glory? Is that what it is?

SAMSON: Does a meat-axe glory in cleaving meat? Does the
jawbone of an ass glory in becoming a blunt instrument?

ELDER: (*Indignantly.*) Come on – away. He has already told us
what is by him. Identity he wants for us. So with identity
let us return to our graves.

RABBI: (*To SAMSON.*) All right then. Go on in your own way. Who can stop you? But at least, Samson, do us one favour. Stop visiting the woman of Sorek. A mad warrior if we have to, the Jews can take. But Delilah – it's not a nice thing, Samson, to know that one is being committed to death by a hero who, even after twenty years, cannot keep his hands off any Gentile woman dangerous enough to amuse him. Shall we go to our graves making excuses for Samson? (*He and the ELDER exit.*)

SAMSON: (*To MANOAH.*) And you, father, no last word of advice from you?

MANOAH: What did I ever have to say to you, my boy? Do what you have to do. Who can do anything else?

SAMSON: I will. I do.

MANOAH: And Samson.

SAMSON: (*Wearily.*) Yes?

MANOAH: Your mother and I loved it the night they caught you not with this Delilah but with the harlot before, the one from Gaza. And you carried from Gaza the stone gates to the top of Mount Hebron. We loved it. Everybody loved it! You know, even when they criticize you and shake their heads and make such a performance over how terrible it all is, what you are doing – our people admire you.

SAMSON: I am grateful for their admiration. I would be more grateful for their active support.

MANOAH: Support is different. Support may get them into even more trouble. But in their hearts, Samson, they support you.

SAMSON: (*Wryly.*) I'll bear it in mind the next time a Philistine spear comes in my direction.

MANOAH: (*Pleading.*) They are Jews, Samson. I know it is difficult sometimes, but it's a duty on us to love all Jews. Try, eh? Soon I'll come to see you again. I'll bring you some of Mother's honey-cakes. All right? And please – try. I must say – you're becoming gentler with the years, my son. You never shouted at them once.

SAMSON: (*Wearily.*) I'm gentle with fatigue. Go in peace, father.

MANOAH: That's right. Peace to everyone – even the
Philistine Jews, eh son?

SAMSON: Peace, peace.

MANOAH: You don't mind my saying so, son, but keep away
a little bit from that Sorek woman. Take it easy, eh? It's
being prophesied here and there by a few of the prophets
that she could be your downfall. For my part it's nothing,
but your mother keeps on the whole time. She completely
disapproves.

SAMSON: I too – totally.

MANOAH: So – take it easy, eh? (*He exits.*)

SCENE TWO: DELILAH'S HOUSE AT SOREK

(*DELILAH is braiding her hair in front of a large bronze mirror
held by a MAID.*)

MAID: So handsome he was, so angry and wild. It's funny how
exciting a man's anger can be.

DELILAH: You gave him my answer as I instructed?

MAID: Exactly. I said, 'My Mistress says that she waits for
her Lord, she longs for her master, she languishes for her
lover.'

DELILAH: You fool. I never said that.

MAID: (*Puzzled.*) But Madam, you did.

DELILAH: I never did. I said: 'I wait for my Lord.'

MAID: So you did. And then afterwards you sighed and spoke
the rest.

DELILAH: But you stupid, stupid girl. The rest I said for
myself – not for him.

MAID: (*Smiles.*) Oh but Madam, it's a great encouragement to
men to hear such things. It makes lions of them. And, oh
that angry young Captain who brought the message, like a
mountain lion he came down to the valley.

DELILAH: Will you please stop exciting yourself over a bad-
tempered little bandit and fix this damned hair for me.

MAID: (*Put out.*) Yes, Madam. (*She fiddles with DELILAH's hair,
adding to her irritation.*)

DELILAH: What is he anyway but a rough, crude, mountain
bandit, middle-aged and overweight?

MAID: (*Thoughtfully.*) I think just a little time with me and he would become quite courtly. These very strong men are often strong simply for fear of being weak, aren't they, my Lady?

DELILAH: (*Impatiently.*) I'm not talking about your little Captain, fool.

MAID: (*Sighs.*) He's not mine, Madam. I'm just dreaming.

DELILAH: Well then, if he's not yours yet after so much dreaming, I really doubt your prowess as a woman. These mountain goats seduce very easily.

MAID: Well, of course, all that fighting and waiting in caves does make them rather eager.

DELILAH: Well then, why do you take so long to bring your little bull to stud?

MAID: He's a funny boy. Keeps telling me I'm unclean. And he, beautiful as he is, stinks like a camel. The life they lead is very unhygienic. There, Madam. Oh that looks beautiful. (*DELILAH studies her hair in the bronze mirror, which the MAID holds up for her, and makes a few minor adjustments.*)

DELILAH: That will do. Leave me now.

(*The MAID bows and exits. DELILAH picks up the mirror and studies herself again.*)

I wait for my Lord. I long for my master, I languish for my lover. (*She puts the mirror down and continues speaking to the audience.*) Why do we say such things? To try and make them true? It's a kind of magic, a sort of praying, a premium on our hopelessness. The truth is that I am the occasional instrument of pleasure of a wild man out of the hills who neither pays me nor protects me, nor offers me even the distant hope of a regular contract. And the fact is that in his absence I am disturbed not because he isn't here, but because he is somewhere else. It isn't his non-existence in my life which ruins everything, but his existence. If only he didn't exist, how then would I long for him and languish for him, but never waste my life waiting for him again. What an unprofitable profession it is to be a mistress. And intensely irksome in a case like this where the wretched man has not even a wife to excuse him. I simply cannot understand what I am doing in such an absurd situation, and yet, is there a woman anywhere who. by her fear of unhappiness, doesn't make even the happiest situations absurdly miserable? How often do we say, 'I only want to be happy' – as if it were a small enough thing to ask of a destiny which, as a general rule, keeps the millions of our insatiable species in a state of chronic unhappiness. But, my god, it's true – I only want to be happy!

(*The MAID enters.*)

He's here so soon?

MAID: No, Madam. It's another gentleman. He's very pressing. Not bad-looking.

DELILAH: Tell him I am engaged.

(*At which point the PHILISTINE NOBLE, previously called the 1ST SUITOR, enters.*)

NOBLE: A woman is never so unengaged as when she waits for her lover.

(*DELILAH indicates to the MAID that she should exit, which she does.*)

DELILAH: Since you are so well informed, Sir, you will also know that it is unsafe for you to be here and will, therefore, excuse my lack of hospitality and leave.

NOBLE: We observe his movements as closely as you do, and there is time. Do you not feel that your entertainment of Samson is a betrayal of our people?

DELILAH: We do not discuss military tactics in bed.

NOBLE: Well, that's a pity then for it's an excellent battleground. (*He studies a tablet in his hand.*) In the past month he has visited you three times. It's a sharp decline of appetite, Madam. After all, do a man's needs vary so sharply?

(*DELILAH, who has her own doubts anyway, now wants only to get definite information.*)

DELILAH: At least take some wine before you go.

NOBLE: Another time when you don't wait so anxiously upon the coming of an occasional friend.

DELILAH: Who is she?

NOBLE: She?

DELILAH: What is it with Samson? Tell me, tell me.

NOBLE: Why should I disturb the serene pool of your contented life?

DELILAH: To hell with your heavy poetics, who is the bitch?

NOBLE: (*Calmly.*) We have no information.

DELILAH: (*Defensively.*) Learn this then – our love is unique.

NOBLE: Come now. Supposing I concede that you are more woman than the run of women, and he more man –

DELILAH: That he certainly is, so leave before your broken neck proves it.

(*The NOBLE continues unconcernedly.*)

NOBLE: In which case the battle between you will be more than ordinary.

DELILAH: Look Sir, if you must have a report for your fellows in Gaza, then tell them that my understanding with the man is perfect, that I am utterly content, deliriously happy and I hope it pleases them. But if it doesn't, let them come here in force, wait with me for my Lord, attend my pleasure with him, and die most violently.

NOBLE: Well spoken. You are a Samsonian patriot. Nevertheless, one who couples with an enemy is not necessarily an enemy.

DELILAH: Once these super-fine Philistine discussions amused me. They always led to undistinguished love-making – but the talk was titillating. (*She sighs.*) I've lost the taste for it.

NOBLE: With what eager regret do women become slaves.

DELILAH: (*Defensively.*) No woman has more ambition than to be the slave of such a man.

NOBLE: Well, then perhaps, since you are so satisfied with it, I will leave you in your slavish insecurity and return when Samson has another slave and you no master. (*He starts to exit.*)

DELILAH: Samson has another?

(*The NOBLE doesn't reply, but he hesitates for a moment. DELILAH confronts him.*)

Do you say he has another?

NOBLE: Our information says that he no longer visits you nightly.

DELILAH: But the campaign has been intense of late.

NOBLE: Indeed the war continues. But formerly he was killing daily, and yet still keeping long and regular nights.

DELILAH: Then why do you plague me, why?

NOBLE: Because the information we have indicates quite clearly – and your aching body cannot deny it, Madam – that the man is growing tired of you.

DELILAH: (*Scornfully.*) He tired? He's tired when he leaves me and at no other time.

NOBLE: Then let us agree that it is taking him longer to recuperate after each visit.

DELILAH: I shall point you out to him, my friend, and watch him smash you like a large blue-fly.

NOBLE: The loyalty of one so certain to be betrayed is most touching. Good night, Madam. I wish you a sweet, if final encounter with your lion.

DELILAH: You know something. What is it you know?

NOBLE: Simply that sooner or later he must betray you.

DELILAH: How do you know it?

NOBLE: From a common experience of the war between our species.

DELILAH: Philistines and Jews are not different species.

NOBLE: But Man and Woman are. Sooner or later he will betray you. Another woman is the least of causes. He has religious mission, professional vocation, historic commitment, crude land-hunger and the pressures of all that he has been and done to drive him forward and away from you. It is more than a regiment of Delilahs.

(*DELILAH is finally overcome and unable to argue.*)

DELILAH: Oh gods yes, it must be so. I know it, I know it.

NOBLE: Then use the only defence a woman has against such male power.

DELILAH: What can I do? I love him.

NOBLE: (*Triumphantly.*) At last, the simple, bitter cry of vulnerable womanhood – the cry that shatters the world around desperate lovers.

DELILAH: I cannot help it.

NOBLE: The rest of the world-shattering cry.

DELILAH: What shall I do?

NOBLE: Betray him first, and totally. Love is a licence for treachery.

DELILAH: Never. (*A pause.*) What is it you ask me to do?

NOBLE: **Entice him and see wherein his great strength lieth, and by what means we may prevail against him that we may bind him to afflict him.**

DELILAH: Oh no, no. Why should I do it?

NOBLE: Because you love him and because you will lose him and because we will give thee, every one of us, eleven hundred pieces of silver. It is not the same as a great love, but, properly invested, it is more permanent.
(*DELILAH is dumbstruck by the awfulness of her interest in the propositions.*)
Do you hear me, lady?

DELILAH: I hear you, serpent. Go glide in the dust forever.
(*The NOBLE smiles, bows slightly, and exits. DELILAH looking at him the while with utter contempt. After he exits her expression changes; she whispers ecstatically.*)
I wait for my Lord, I long for my master, I languish for my lover. (*With furious venom.*) The lying, treacherous, hateful, randy dog! (*Her mood changes again. She appears to be calculating.*) Eleven hundred pieces of silver each from one thousand Philistine nobles – why, that's nearly a million. More than a million. About a million. (*Desperately.*) Gods, if only I could be certain he would love me forever, I would not sell him for the world. But what man's love lasts forever? And a thousand times eleven hundred – yes, it is more than a million. (*She calculates thoughtfully as she turns to fix her hair, studying herself in the bronze mirror. She is very thoughtful.*)

SCENE THREE: OUTSIDE DELILAH'S HOUSE

(*The MAID sits on her haunches, waiting. She starts and gets to her feet as SAMSON, accompanied by DAN, a young Captain, enters.*)

MAID: Who is it?
(*DAN has his drawn sword in his hand.*)

DAN: It is the man from the hills.

(*The MAID bows.*)

MAID: My Mistress waits for her Lord.

SAMSON: Thank you. (*To DAN.*) Don't hang around all night,
my boy. There's no danger here.

DAN: (*Stubbornly.*) I will keep guard.

(*SAMSON smiles, shrugs, nods to the MAID and enters Delilah's
house. DAN stands stiffly on guard. The MAID looks him up and
down admiringly.*)

MAID: Will you spend the whole night here, Captain, I mean
just standing there with that terrifying sword?

DAN: I will do my duty, woman.

MAID: Oh yes, I know. You always do, and I really admire
you for it. But it gets very cold here at nights in this season.
I'll bring you a little wine to warm you.

DAN: You don't seem ever to understand, woman. I am a
Nazarite like my lord. We don't drink wine.

MAID: Of course. How stupid of me. (*She laughs.*) It just seems
so funny that people should have moral principles about
keeping warm at night.

DAN: (*Impatiently.*) That's not the point. Oh I can't explain.

MAID: Well, I would never understand anyway. Is it all right
for you to keep warm in my tent?

DAN: (*Surlily.*) Thank you, but it won't be necessary.

(*The MAID now approaches DAN and, standing close to him,
looks up into his face charmingly. He looks away from her, staring
towards his duty.*)

MAID: I know that Nazarites are allowed to go with women.

DAN: (*Angrily.*) Of course we are.

MAID: (*Laughs.*) Perhaps you would like me to find you a
woman for the night. (*She laughs again.*) It is an excellent
way of keeping warm.

DAN: (*Roughly.*) It is not necessary – but I thank you.

MAID: Oh, please don't bother. It's only common hospitality.
I mean, I know that we are unclean and all that but I could
find you a woman and make her bathe. Would that be all
right?

DAN: I tried to explain to you last time. Unclean doesn't mean that you need a bath.

MAID: Oh yes, I do remember. I am so stupid. Would *you* like a bath? I know you don't get many opportunities up there in those wild hills.

DAN: (*Doubtfully.*) Well – a bath would be pleasant.

MAID: (*Eagerly.*) Oh, wonderful. I'll prepare it for you myself. I prepare the most beautiful baths. My Mistress is mad about them. And I scrub and massage delightfully.

DAN: Thank you but that won't be necessary.

MAID: Oh, please don't worry about it. It's part of our law of hospitality. We just cannot allow a stranger to take a bath on his own. Now, you keep guard there and I'll make everything ready for us. Oh, it's such a beautiful night. Though, of course, it will get very, very cold.

(*The MAID exits leaving DAN somewhat uncertain about what he has committed himself to.*)

SCENE FOUR: DELILAH'S HOUSE

(*SAMSON and DELILAH lie together on a great couch of fur-skins.*)

DELILAH: Do you love me?

(*SAMSON doesn't reply.*)

Oh, how I love my Lord!

(*SAMSON stirs irritably.*)

Are you well my Lord?

(*SAMSON sighs, or grunts, or both.*)

Can I bring my Lord something? Something to drink? Would my Lord eat? (*She gently strokes his shoulders.*) How hard and knotted are my Lord's muscles. I shall massage your shoulders. Turn about.

(*SAMSON gets up from the couch, frustrating her.*)

SAMSON: I must leave.

DELILAH: So soon?

SAMSON: I must.

DELILAH: But why so soon? What battles will you direct in the middle of the night? Stay till morning I beg of you.

SAMSON: I must away.

DELILAH: (*Scornfully.*) What do you know of love?

SAMSON: Delilah – not that old debate. I love you and you have comforted and restored me. My mind is clear again. I see the way I must go. And so I leave you with love in my heart.

DELILAH: So leaving is proof of loving?

SAMSON: Say no more, Lady. I'll stay.

DELILAH: Should I kiss the hem of that stinking ill-cured ancient lionskin in gratitude?

SAMSON: You ask me to stay and so I stay. What more?

DELILAH: (*Furiously.*) Will you not stay because you want it, and not because I ask it?

SAMSON: You'll break my mind, sweetheart, with these everlasting riddles. Come to bed. I'll stay till the hour before sunrise.

DELILAH: No.

SAMSON: No?

DELILAH: Go now.

SAMSON: You want me to go?

DELILAH: (*Uncertainly.*) Yes.

SAMSON: Why then I'll go.

DELILAH: Before you go –

SAMSON: Yes?

DELILAH: Answer me one simple question, simply.

SAMSON: Yes.

DELILAH: Do you love me?

SAMSON: Is this a simple question to be answered between the middle of the night and the hour before dawn?

DELILAH: (*Bursts out.*) It's a question that can be answered in the movement of an eye or the sighing of a breath.

SAMSON: Tonight my breath rattled like a hunted gazelle. So, it is proven I love you. Will I leave or shall we to bed again?

DELILAH: (*Irritatedly.*) Oh, do as you want.

SAMSON: (*Too reasonably.*) But I would do what you want, my honey creature – if you could make up your mind.

DELILAH: (*Pleadingly.*) Oh Samson, my soul would rest for ever if I did but surely know you loved me. Prove, love, that you love me.

(*SAMSON takes in this fundamental female request slowly and turns to the audience, who remember with him another woman earlier in the story who made the same request – and its consequences.*)

SAMSON: (*To audience.*) Familiar, isn't it? From the first woman to the last, the same impossible demand echoes, an unanswerable question, the cry of a lamb to the rocks. (*He turns to DELILAH.*) Sweet lamb of Sorek, how shall I prove it? Can a man dam up the anxious disbelief of a woman who is incapable of loving herself? And if he does contain it, that irritating trickle of uncertainty, will it not in the end burst its banks and drown him?

(*DELILAH doesn't reply.*)

(*With gentle resignation.*) All right then. Tell me, love, how shall I prove love? (*To audience.*) Now it comes. It comes now.

DELILAH: **Tell me Lord, I pray thee, wherein thy great strength lieth and wherewith thou mightest be bound to afflict thee.**

SAMSON: (*To audience.*) For answering this question I am remembered in history as a man only. (*Turns to DELILAH.*) **If thou bind me with seven green withies that were never dried, then shall I be weak and be as another man.**

DELILAH: (*Unbelievingly.*) Seven green withies?

SAMSON: Alternatively, maybe I'm just a very powerful man. Did this explanation ever occur to you?

DELILAH: Of course. You must be extraordinary otherwise I wouldn't feel this extraordinary love for you.

SAMSON: (*Hopefully.*) Can we leave the question then, and go to bed?

DELILAH: Maybe. No – there must be some magic as well. After all you don't exercise regularly, your diet is short on protein, you don't drink wine, and you're too dependent on sex and violence to be a holy man. (*Impatiently.*) Tell me the secret, Samson. Prove you love me.

SAMSON: (*Resignedly.*) Seven green withies.

DELILAH: (*Eagerly.*) I think there are seven here somewhere.

(*She goes off to look for them.*)

SAMSON: (*To audience.*) I know that there are men lying in wait about the tent. They wait while my guard takes his bath and I answer Love's deadly catechism.

(*DELILAH returns, she mimes a bunch of withies and mimes again her binding of SAMSON with them.*)

(*Mildly to DELILAH.*) Supposing there are enemies lying in wait?

DELILAH: My love protects you.

SAMSON: Supposing it fails?

DELILAH: Are you afraid to test it?

SAMSON: Anyone who cares for his love should be afraid to test her.

(*DELILAH kneels to bind his legs.*)

DELILAH: Tell me if I hurt you.

SAMSON: You will, you will.

(*DELILAH finishes binding his legs.*)

DELILAH: (*Delightedly.*) Who would have thought it? Seven green withies. (*She is suddenly alarmed.*) What sound was that?

SAMSON: (*Mildly.*) It's the sound of the men lying in wait.

DELILAH: (*Hysterically.*) **The Philistines be upon thee Samson!**

(*SAMSON is miming his bound hands and legs. Now he mimes breaking the withies.*)

(*Aghast.*) **You broke the withies as a thread of tow is broken when it toucheth the fire.** (*She calls.*) **His strength is not known!**

(*The sound offstage of the men lying in wait subsides at her signal.*)

SAMSON: I believe you have something to say to me.

DELILAH: (*With suppressed, hurt fury.*)

Behold thou hast mocked me and told me lies. Thou lovest me not.

(*She throws herself down on the couch distraught. SAMSON turns to the audience.*)

SAMSON: (*To audience.*) There are two overwhelming questions in my story. The first is, what is God doing? We shall continue to examine this question after the present tableau reaches its inevitable conclusion. The second is, what am I doing? I know she will betray me, I lie again, but in the end I will tell her and it will be so.

(*To DELILAH.*) **If they bind me fast with new ropes that were never occupied, then shall I be weak and be as other men.**

DELILAH: (*Eagerly.*) I'll bring new ropes.

SAMSON: (*To audience.*) Later the lies become a little wild.

(*To DELILAH.*) **If thou weavest the seven locks of my head with the web, then shall I be weak and be as other men.**

(*DELILAH turns on him furiously.*)

DELILAH: I'm sick of it.

How canst thou say 'I love thee' when thy heart is not with me? Thou hast mocked me these three times and hast not told me wherein thy great strength lieth. How canst thou say 'I love thee' when thy heart is not with me? How canst thou say 'I love thee'? How canst thou say 'I love'? How canst thou say? How canst thou? How canst? How? (*DELILAH continues to mime the questions endlessly.*)

SAMSON: (*Wearily.*)

She presses daily with her words so that my soul is vexed unto death.

DELILAH: How canst thou say 'I love thee'? How canst thou say 'I love'? How canst thou say? How canst thou?

SAMSON: Enough! My soul is vexed unto death.

DELILAH: How canst thou say 'I love thee'? How canst thou say? How canst thou? How?

SAMSON: Enough! Enough!

DELILAH: How canst?

(*SAMSON seizes her and puts his hand over her mouth.*)

SAMSON: So here is my heart, woman. Eat it.

There hath not come a razor upon my head for I have been a Nazarite unto God from my mother's womb. If I be shaven then my strength will go from me and I shall become weak and like any other man.

DELILAH: Is that all?

SAMSON: That's all.

DELILAH: (*Sullenly.*) I don't believe it.

SAMSON: It's true.

DELILAH: You're making a fool of me again.

SAMSON: That's my secret.

DELILAH: You don't love me. You never loved me. I shall go away.

SAMSON: (*Wearily.*) Go – stay. Believe or not. My soul is vexed unto death.

DELILAH: Not too tired to come to bed, I expect.

SAMSON: Go to. I will follow.

DELILAH: (*Triumphantly.*) Tonight we shall lie with a razor between us.

SAMSON: Go to. Let me think awhile on what we are about.
(*DELILAH exits.*)
(*To audience.*) I am a tired lion with a compulsion to eat honey. I see it there golden, luminous and infinitely satisfying. And I must eat to satiate my ravenous leonine soul which afterwards will purr and sleep for a little, till waking it roars in agony of need for honey once again. In less poetic terms I am addicted to her and deprived must sustain acutely painful symptoms of withdrawal; an idiotic male syndrome. But I have an excuse. As God's instrument I can attribute all that happens to me to His obscure intentions. Has God a god to provide Him with such an excuse? (*He yawns profoundly.*) Exhausting. isn't it?
(*He sighs and rests on the couch and falls asleep. DELILAH re-enters. She studies him for a moment.*)

DELILAH: All men look pitiful asleep, pale, troubled, breathing hard and stupid. As an act of belief I tell myself that this heavy sleeper is a mythical lover for whom I forsook my people and my gods. I prayed to him as he bore down on me. Satisfy me. Fill me. Shoot me full of your honey, for I am empty again. Fill me, great roaring heart, fill the cold and empty moon below my breasts with hot honey of the sun, my lion. Bear down on me, my beast –
(*A Philistine BARBER enters tentatively as she speaks.*)
What the hell do you want?

BARBER: You called for a barber, Lady.

DELILAH: Was that what it was, my remembered ecstasy – a call for a barber?

BARBER: I thought I heard a call, Lady. Though his lordship there is not exactly prone to my art. He is a hairy gentleman, isn't he, my lady? Beautiful head of hair. Too good for a gentleman really. Looks to me as if he'll keep it right into his old age. The follicles have a strong appearance. People don't realize how diet affects the hair.

(*DELILAH seems dazed as the BARBER chatters on.*)

DELILAH: You have a razor?

BARBER: Of course, my Lady. As my old father used to say, one of the best-known barbers in Gaza he was, 'Whether you be barber, soldier or just a fool, never travel without your tool.' He was a bit coarse the old fellow but a first-class barber, may he rest in peace. I wish I was half as good.

DELILAH: Give me the razor.

BARBER: Give it to you, my Lady?

DELILAH: Give it to me.

(*The BARBER produces his razor from his bag.*)

BARBER: This is my beard razor. For the hair you don't need it so sharp. Which was his lordship thinking of having trimmed?

(*DELILAH deeply absorbed and very tensely, with adoration and ambivalence, holds the razor in one hand and gently draws up the long locks of SAMSON's hair with the other.*)

DELILAH: Are these the strings that bind me to a man?

(*The BARBER is watching her curiously.*)

BARBER: It could well be, Lady. A lot of ladies are much affected by a gentleman's fine hair.

DELILAH: (*Without looking at him.*) Get out.

BARBER: What do you say, Lady?

(*DELILAH looks at him with coldly murderous venom. The BARBER backs away frightened but persistent.*)

You surely won't do the job yourself, my Lady? It's a small trade but skilled withal. A bad haircut can mar a gentleman's appearance and ruin his chances for life. It's a dangerous weapon in the wrong hands, Lady.

DELILAH: (*Quietly.*) Then it will cut a fool's throat.
(*The BARBER sees that she means it and backs away hurriedly.*)
BARBER: Do it, Lady, if the fancy has taken you. I'll not say a
word. I'm a good union man but I'll not say a word.
(*He backs off stage. DELILAH looks back at SAMSON. Her eyes
look slowly across his body from his feet to his head. She gently
takes the seven locks of his hair in her hand. She kneels and
touches them with her cheek and her lips.*)
DELILAH: Ah love! (*With deep feeling.*) Love! (*Then holding the
seven locks in one hand she cuts them one by one.*) Love! Love!
Love! Love! Love! Love! Love!
(*Then as she looks at the seven locks in her hand horror strikes
her, her hand opens and she drops them to the floor. Then the
razor drops.*)
(*With deep grief.*) Ah love.
(*SAMSON wakes suddenly from his sleep.*)
SAMSON: (*Alarmed.*) The Philistines are upon me! (*He sees her
and his frightened expression fades and he smiles.*) Ah Delilah!
DELILAH: **The Philistines are upon thee, Samson!**
SAMSON: (*Still smiling.*) Not again. You would not play so bad
a joke again.
DELILAH: (*With mounting hysteria.*) It wasn't true, was it? You
lied to me, didn't you, didn't you lie to me? Say you did.
Please tell me it was a lie.
SAMSON: (*Puzzled.*) What?
DELILAH: The hair. The hair.
(*She looks down at his locks on the floor. He follows her gaze.
His face drains of blood. He looks back at her slowly and she
knows now, finally, both that he loves her and that he is lost. As
they look at one another with the growing terror of lovers whose
loss is irrecoverable, the Lords of the Philistines, heavily armed.
silently enter barring SAMSON's retreat.
End of Act Two.*)

Act Three

SCENE ONE: MANOAH'S HOUSE

(*MANOAH dictates to the SCRIBE who writes laboriously on a parchment.*)

MANOAH: Read it back.

SCRIBE: And she said, 'The Philistines be upon thee, Samson.'

MANOAH: Yes. That's right. 'And he woke out of his sleep.'

SCRIBE: (*Writing.*) 'And he woke…' Do you have to say 'out of his sleep'? If he woke it's clear he was asleep.

MANOAH: To me it sounds better to say 'And he woke out of his sleep.'

SCRIBE: I'm just making a suggestion that's all.

MANOAH: I'm grateful for your suggestions, but please take it down my way. So – 'He woke out of his sleep.'
(*The SCRIBE shrugs and writes as SAMSON'S MOTHER enters. She seems much older, broken and perhaps a little unhinged. She wears mourning. Her tone is bitter and querulous.*)

MOTHER: (*Argumentively.*) His hair cut so a girl with no breasts could lead him to the place of execution.

MANOAH: (*Patiently.*) We are working, my dear.

MOTHER: I taught him this.

MANOAH: Yes. True. But now we are working.

MOTHER: Oh, my boy Samson, what a judge you were, except for those women.

SCRIBE: (*Aside to MANOAH.*) Maybe I should take the opportunity to cut some fresh pens. Once she starts –

MANOAH: Good idea.
(*The SCRIBE exits.*)

MOTHER: And now where is he? Lying in the filth with the fleas nesting in his hair stubble!

MANOAH: Make some cheese. Bake. Do something. It will take your mind off.
(*SAMSON'S MOTHER, totally involved in her emotions, ignores him.*)

MOTHER: Those filthy, uncircumcised pigs with that secret weapon of theirs, that rotten lousy Dagonish priestess, that sacred prostitute, that Delilah! (*She spits out three times.*)

MANOAH: Easy, easy, mother.

MOTHER: Easy? Easy! When everything is broken in little pieces around him? When the whole world comes down on him, there is left only his mother. Should she be easy?

MANOAH: We've been over it before. So often. For a whole year nothing else.

(*She suddenly seems calm and with a slightly insane comprehension.*)

MOTHER: You know what it is?

MANOAH: What is it?

MOTHER: This whole life of his is a sermon.

MANOAH: So, good. Leave me to write it and perhaps by the time I've finished I'll see the message and so it'll be a proper sermon. All right?

MOTHER: Oh no! This is not the end, with him rotting quietly in a dungeon with a mouse for company and the fleas biting. This is no end for a son of mine, for a hero – one whose birth was prophesied, who was raised in purity, who never had a knife touch his hair until that dirty whore got him into her clutches!

MANOAH: (*Wearily.*) I remember, believe me, I remember.

MOTHER: The world will remember for ever. They will curse her for ever. They will call him an idiot for ever.

MANOAH: Enough, woman.

MOTHER: Never!

MANOAH: (*Roars.*) Do you hear me, woman? I say enough!

MOTHER: (*Sullenly.*) From me you'll hear nothing. What should I say now?

MANOAH: All right then. So let's get on with it. (*He looks around for the SCRIBE.*) Oh, where has he gone?

MOTHER: I mean, did I say something when, as a boy, he came to you and said he wanted the woman from Timnath? Did I say anything then?

MANOAH: Yes. You said why can't he marry a Jewish girl. So did I. But he didn't. He couldn't. It was his destiny.

MOTHER: I said, of course, I said. He was my only son, born when I had for years given up all hope of conceiving. Naturally, I said.

MANOAH: We know, we know the whole story. Everybody knows it.

MOTHER: (*Persists.*) When he was a little boy with long hair and everybody was saying 'Please, it's time Samson had a haircut. It looks ridiculous! He looks like a girl.' You don't know how I felt. I did my duty. I kept my vow to the angel. I wanted a little boy like other little boys. But no. I kept my word.

MANOAH: And he paid for it. You think it's easy to wear long hair in a short-haired society?

MOTHER: All right. It was hard for him too. But we of Israel are not for ourselves. We are for each other and for Jahveh. Hear, oh Israel, the Lord, thy God, the Lord is One!

MANOAH: So He heard and now *he* wakes up in darkness.

MOTHER: (*Stubbornly.*) Jahveh is with him still.

MANOAH: (*Sighs.*) I'm not so sure. Jahveh hates the weak.

MOTHER: It'll be all right in the end, you'll see. After all, what did he do that was so terrible? He loved a Philistine girl, that's all. Fool, with the career he had before him, the opportunities – thrown away for 'love'.

MANOAH: At his age love is a desperate illness. For a middle-aged judge, passion is fatal.

MOTHER: (*Stubbornly.*) Only because the girl was a Philistine. If she was an Israelite girl his hair would be twice as long, he would be twice as strong, he would kill twice as many Philistines and Israel would be master of the world. That's because a Jewish wife is a help to her husband.

MANOAH: How can you help who you fall in love with? I mean, don't take this wrong – but that angel of yours –

MOTHER: (*Immediately on the defensive.*) My angel was a proper angel sent by Jahveh. It's in the annals of the tribe now. It's history, Manoah. Nobody argues with Jewish history. Oh, he came like a prince, like a prince he came. In a long white silk robe with his fine brown lean features and his brilliant black eyes…

MANOAH: (*Sighs.*) She's right. Who argues with Jewish history?

MOTHER: (*Carried away.*) And I was working in the fields, a slave, like all our people. And suddenly he stood – his

back to the shimmering sunlight, a vision, a mirage. And
I was tired from the heat and the work and the long years
without children. But I was handsome. Of eight sisters, I
was the most beautiful. And there I was, twenty-four, a
middle-aged woman already, but still handsome, and he
looked at me and his face shone like the sun and I was
blinded. And he spoke the words of prophesy and I fainted
there in the burning sunlight. (*She seems to sink a little,
reliving her ecstasy.*)

MANOAH: So you fainted.

MOTHER: (*Defensively.*) In such circumstances, any woman
would faint. What's so wrong?

MANOAH: I don't really want to discuss it now.

MOTHER: What's to discuss? A mother-to-be has a visitation
from an angel. What's so unusual?

MANOAH: (*Warily.*) Nothing, nothing.

MOTHER: (*Threateningly.*) This isn't the first time you've said
something against my angel. Are you daring to deny the
prophesy? Is that what's behind all our trouble? Is that why
Samson is in this absolutely tragic situation?

MANOAH: Did I say something? I said nothing, nothing.

MOTHER: (*Bitterly.*) My son, a hero of forty-two, a little bit
overweight, but still a hero, captured by the Philistines, but
nevertheless a hero, sold into slavery to pigs by a cheap
priestess of a low-down sex-god, but still a hero in Israel.
And this hero's father dares to have doubts about his wife's
angel. A pure Jewish angel, and *he* dares to have doubts!

MANOAH: (*Firmly.*) All right. You want the truth? He never
did sound too Jewish to me. He –

MOTHER: (*Appalled.*) What? You're saying my angel was
a foreign angel? A Gentile angel? You can say that to a
mother in Israel? Oh, woe is me! (*She starts to cry a little bit.*)

MANOAH: (*Firmly.*) Now you listen to me. You wanted this
discussion. So let's have it out at last. This long white silk
robe, this dark skin, these piercing black eyes, this fine
aquiline nose – this is how the Philistine nobility look, isn't
it?

MOTHER: (*Hysterically covering her ears.*) I don't want to discuss it any more!

MANOAH: (*Decisively.*) I am not, my dear, questioning the sincerity of your faith, but maybe this angel actually was a Philistine noble. He's riding past the fields, he sees a beautiful Israelite woman bending over, he has an idea he would like to know her better...

MOTHER: (*Crying.*) Blasphemer! Father of a girl-chaser! How can you say such terrible things?

MANOAH: All right then. What was the angel's name?

MOTHER: An angel has to introduce himself formally? He didn't give a name.

MANOAH: (*Shrugs.*) I'm a simple shepherd of the tribe of Dan. What do I know about angels?

MOTHER: (*Crying.*) I'm going. I'm leaving. I won't stay here to be told I'm a loose woman and my son a bastard! God forgive me for being a woman and a mother!

MANOAH: (*Shrugs.*) So. Go.

(*The SCRIBE enters.*)

SCRIBE: (*To MANOAH.*) She's going?

(*About to leave, SAMSON'S MOTHER turns on MANOAH violently.*)

MOTHER: And another thing!

SCRIBE: (*Hurriedly.*) I'll come back later. (*He hurries off.*)

MOTHER: This is a boy who tore lions to pieces with his bare hands. Is that normal?

MANOAH: The whole thing was never normal.

MOTHER: This is a young man who carried the stone gates of Gaza to the top of Mount Hebron. That's a long way to carry a stone gate.

MANOAH: (*Impatiently.*) Who's arguing about that?

MOTHER: (*Triumphantly.*) All right then. You'll admit that only those favoured by Jahveh can do such things.

MANOAH: I'll admit it wasn't normal.

MOTHER: (*Conclusively.*) So. What's wrong with my angel?

MANOAH: Question.

MOTHER: (*Grandly.*) If you wish.

MANOAH: Where was he going this boy when he tore the lion to pieces?

MOTHER: You expect me to remember every little detail?

MANOAH: (*Triumphantly.*) He was going to make love with the Woman of Timnath. That's where.

MOTHER: So, a boy's high-spirited. What's so terrible?

MANOAH: As for the gates of Gaza –

MOTHER: (*Proudly.*) That will be remembered for ever. What a performance!

MANOAH: But it will also be remembered that on that night he was caught sleeping with a harlot at Gaza.

MOTHER: Treacherous bitch! She also sold him to the Philistines. But he destroyed them every last one and for a joke carried away their gate. (*She laughs.*) In those days he was always full of jokes and riddles and fun.

MANOAH: (*Resignedly.*) You miss the point.

MOTHER: The point is, my son is a Jewish hero and nothing else matters.

MANOAH: (*Almost to himself.*) But when the Timnath woman betrayed him why didn't he learn? How can I explain this?

MOTHER: She was the one who told them the answer. Out of whatever it was came forth something or other. I can't remember the exact details.

MANOAH: Strength. And sweetness. Maybe that's the answer. Jahveh gave him the strength but he had to take the sweetness. For who can live by strength alone?

MOTHER: (*Contemptuously.*) Sweet little slut, that one from Timnath, who giggled a lot.

MANOAH: (*Sighs.*) She did and she burned for it. She was fifteen.

MOTHER: (*Savagely.*) All Philistines should die at such an age.

MANOAH: All love should die at such an age. Later on it kills you.

MOTHER: (*Impatiently.*) Listen! I can't stand here talking with you all day. The older you get the more you talk. Talk. Talk. Talk. I've got things to get on with.

MANOAH: I talk?

MOTHER: (*Aggressively.*) You want to talk or you want to eat? If you want to eat let me get on with it. I don't talk. I do. That's Jewish.

(*She exits busily. MANOAH sighs deeply, shakes his head and turns his attention back to the writing on the table. The SCRIBE comes in.*)

SCRIBE: She's really gone?

MANOAH: (*Impatiently.*) Your writing is terrible. Read it back to me.

(*The SCRIBE bends over the parchment and reads.*)

SCRIBE: 'And he woke out of his sleep.' (*He shrugs distastefully at the phrase.*)

MANOAH: Now! 'And she said, "The Philistines be upon thee, Samson." And he woke out of his sleep and said, "I will go out as at other times before and shake myself."'

(*The SCRIBE stops writing and looks at MANOAH questioningly.*)

(*Testily.*) Why are you stopping now?

SCRIBE: 'Shake myself.' I don't like 'shake myself.'

MANOAH: Put it down, put it down. You can make the refinements later. What?

SCRIBE: 'I will go out as at other times before and shake myself.'

MANOAH: That's right. 'And he wist not that the Lord was departed from him.'

(*The SCRIBE takes it down.*)

'But the Philistines took him and… (*He hesitates.*) …and…'

SCRIBE: (*Gently.*) I know. I know.

MANOAH: (*Firmly.*) 'And put out his eyes and brought him down to Gaza and bound him with fetters of brass and he did grind in the prison house.'

SCRIBE: (*Writing.*) 'And he did grind in the prison house.' (*The SCRIBE sighs deeply.*) So, that's how it ends.

MANOAH: No. It is not ended yet. But put it down.

SCRIBE: It's down. It's down.

(*The sound of distant grinding is heard.*)

SCENE TWO: THE PRISON HOUSE IN GAZA

(*In the prison house below the Temple of Dagon in Gaza, SAMSON sits in pillowed comfort in clean robes, unfettered, smoking a water-pipe, being attended by a young GIRL in the white silk dress of a novitiate. He is relaxed, overweight, degenerate and neatly blinded, his eyes beautiful and empty after an expert surgical operation to remove the optic nerves.*)

SAMSON: It draws badly. Blow on the coal.

GIRL: Yes, Sir. (*She blows gently on the coals beneath the pipe.*)

SAMSON: How old are you?

GIRL: Fifteen. Is the pipe drawing better now, Sir?

(*SAMSON draws on the pipe and stares at her sightlessly.*)

You eat me with your blind eyes, Sir.

SAMSON: Come closer.

(*The GIRL comes closer. SAMSON feels for her throat.*)

GIRL: (*Embarrassed.*) I know you're used to much better than me, sir. I know it's a fantastic honour for me. I know I don't deserve it. But my mother is very ambitious for me, and I will try very hard, sir.

(*SAMSON's hand is feeling the GIRL's face.*)

SAMSON: (*Preoccupied.*) Over this another and behind this another. Where is the ultimate face?

GIRL: I'm supposed to be quite pretty, Sir. I mean, I don't think I am. But a lot of the pilgrims say I am. (*She sighs.*) Of course men always say that when they want you. You can't really take it seriously. But I *think* I'm *quite* pretty.

SAMSON: Where is the ultimate face? (*He withdraws his hand hopelessly from her face and turns his blind eyes away.*)

GIRL: Well, I think I am it actually. That is why mother wanted it to be me. That is why she gave great gifts to the priests. (*Proudly.*) I am the thousandth woman dedicated to the god.

SAMSON: Have there been a thousand of you?

GIRL: Oh yes. And all conceived. I think you're marvellous. We all do.

SAMSON: In war and sex everyone lies.

GIRL: (*Overwhelmed.*) I am the thousandth bride of God's Prick. It's wonderful.

SAMSON: What did you call me?

GIRL: I'm sorry, Sir. Did I say something wrong? I mean, 'Revered Phallus of Omnipotent Dagon' is a bit difficult for the ordinary people. And God's Prick is sort of homey. When I have your son, Sir, I will call him after you.

SAMSON: Thank you. But can you be sure it will be a son?

GIRL: (*Alarmed.*) Oh, it must be. The girls are sacrificed immediately. But the boys are brought up in a special school to be warriors, supermen, through whose strength our people will be forever unconquerable. (*Urgently.*) Oh, please Sir, will you not lay with me now? I die for you. Kill me, Sir. Make me live, Sir. Do it quickly. Now. Now.

SAMSON: Smoke a little first.

(*He hands her the pipe. The GIRL draws on it greedily.*)
(*Muses.*) So I, a blunt instrument of Destiny, the secret weapon of Jahveh, have become God's Prick. (*He laughs.*) There's a joke there somewhere.

GIRL: Oh – this is strong.

SAMSON: Smoke, smoke.

GIRL: Is it usual, sir?

SAMSON: Essential.

GIRL: I wish for the sake of my mother to do everything well, Sir.

SAMSON: I'm sure you will.

GIRL: Thank you. (*Shyly.*) You knew my mother well once, Sir.

SAMSON: (*Yawning.*) Was she – a temple girl?

GIRL: (*Indignantly.*) Certainly not, Sir. She was the Great Harlot of Gaza, and for her sake you did the impossible, bearing on your back the stone gates of the city to the crest of Mount Hebron. (*Proudly.*) Did ever a woman receive a greater compliment than that?

SAMSON: So you are the daughter of that great priestess?

GIRL: (*With simple pride.*) I am, Sir. And one day, if I am good, I will be as great a whore as she has been. She's retired now, an old woman of nearly forty but still does good work for the god. She conducts the finishing school at our temple and speaks often of the monument you raised to her.

SAMSON: (*His curiosity aroused.*) Does she also speak of how she betrayed me to the Philistines, and how I killed very many of them?

GIRL: (*Indignantly.*) Certainly not, Sir. My mother is a woman and prefers to remember only the nicer things. Your superb compliment to her is the poor lady's sweetest memory. She was very upset about you and Delilah. She said Delilah wasn't professional. (*Impatiently.*) Oh please lay with me now, Sir. If you don't it will be my first black mark and I do so want to be professional.

SAMSON: Come, alien, let me help you in your eternal homework.

GIRL: (*Delightedly.*) Oh, thank you, Sir. (*Ecstatically.*) You are the greatest lover of my great harlot mother. How happy she will be when I tell her I pleased you well. (*She starts to embrace him very expertly.*)

SAMSON: Oh yes. Your little teeth are cunning, little bitch-fox.

GIRL: If I please you greatly, Sir, will you reward me?

SAMSON: Of course – with a son, a super-warrior.

GIRL: (*Subtly.*) Yes, of course. But will you also tell me some little secret?

SAMSON: You too!

GIRL: (*Eagerly.*) Tell me, tell me. Then I shall make you happy beyond the memory of all the others.
(*She embraces him eagerly. SAMSON, jaded as he is, begins to respond, when the GIRL withdraws.*)
(*Accusingly.*) You do respond somewhat readily, Sir. Is it for my particular taste or smell? Or is it quite impersonal? (*She is obviously a little hurt.*)

SAMSON: (*Kindly.*) No, no. It is not entirely impersonal. Go on.
(*The GIRL continues her lovemaking and then stops again.*)
(*Irritably.*) Well, what is it, child?

GIRL: I have been calculating, Sir. You have been here a year or so and for me to be the thousandth privileged one calculates a daily turnover of three such.

SAMSON: I assure you, sweet girl, few of them were as accomplished as you. Now go to it. Smoke, smoke.
(*The GIRL smokes resentfully.*)

GIRL: (*Petulantly.*) Well, I think it's all a little impersonal. (*She brightens.*) Unless you see me with your touch. Is it so?

SAMSON: (*Edgily.*) Blindness does sharpen the touch and intensify the imagination.

GIRL: (*Much relieved and affected by the smoke.*) Oh – I am so very happy. (*She smokes again, swoons and moans.*) Now – now – now – now.

(*She faints away. SAMSON sighs and claps his hands. ZOAB, a young Philistine priest, enters.*)

SAMSON: Ah, Amnon, here is another for you.

ZOAB: Amnon is off duty today. I am Zoab.

SAMSON: You are new to this post, Zoab?

(*ZOAB is very refined and highly intellectual, and somewhat pompous.*)

ZOAB: I come straight from the seminary, Sir.

SAMSON: (*Wryly.*) Good. You should be in excellent condition for the work. Take this child and service her well. I had a little trouble and much joy of her mother.

ZOAB: Yes, sir. Of course I will – but – (*He looks at the GIRL and hesitates.*)

SAMSON: Well, go to it, lad. There are more waiting.

ZOAB: There aren't actually, Sir. This one will complete the cycle. There will be a great feast in your honour with great sacrifices to the Lord Dagon.

SAMSON: Good, good. Go to it, go.

ZOAB: Certainly, Sir. May I ask a question first, Sir?

SAMSON: (*Sighs.*) Another intellectual. Can I stop you?

ZOAB: Thank you, Sir. The question of your extraordinary strength, Sir, which for some twenty years was a *casus belli* between our peoples –

SAMSON: (*Wearily.*) Must we go into it yet again? Your woman Delilah found the secret, sold it for more than she could count and keeps – I believe – my hair as a souvenir of our short but incredibly beautiful friendship. What more is there to be said?

ZOAB: We Philistines are a rational people, Sir. We find it very difficult to swallow the extraordinary myths which are the daily bread of your strange, stubborn, perverse and dangerous tribe.

SAMSON: Is it easier to believe in the strength of a fishtailed idol of gold, saturated in dolphin oil and presiding over a continuous orgy of nymphomanic priestesses and exhausted pilgrims?

ZOAB: Oh, much easier. Our Dagon reminds us that without fertility there is nothing. Our priestesses lay with the unhappy stranger to show us that the grim wastage of life may be forgotten in the fertile transports of a joy without which living would be too dreary a process to continue. Our religion is a simple and scientific poetry. You can hardly say the same for yours.

SAMSON: I say nothing for mine. Religion and sex have never interested me very much.

ZOAB: But theology, wool and puritanism are the principal products of Israel.

SAMSON: (*Irritably.*) My boy, I am a middle-aged folk hero who has lost his home following. Excuse me your debate, do your job and preserve my myth.

ZOAB: (*Thoughtfully.*) Of course, of course. We support your myth for good reasons. After the surprise of our discovery that you were impotent –

SAMSON: (*Impatiently.*) It went with the hair. Some sort of traumatic shock, your doctors thought.

ZOAB: (*Irritatingly.*) Of course, of course. No one has ever implied that you were always so –

SAMSON: (*Roars.*) Ask Delilah!

ZOAB: (*Calmly.*) Well, her evidence was discounted. Women lie about the potency of their men. It flatters their narcissism.

SAMSON: (*Stiffly.*) May I remind you of the occasion on which I killed one thousand of your people with the jawbone of an ass?

ZOAB: This has been carefully researched. The actual number of dead was fourteen.

SAMSON: You record your figure, boy, and we will record ours. Let's see which one history remembers.

ZOAB: (*Undisturbed.*) In any case, Sir, military prowess invariably travels with erotic disinclination. The great military leaders who have not been actual pederasts have been, by and large, sexually neuter.

SAMSON: (*Furious.*) Is it the intention of your diabolical inquisitors to drive me mad with the jejune maunderings of a seminary theoretician?

ZOAB: I assure you, Sir, there is nothing personal in my observations. But we do have to consider your future.

SAMSON: (*Wearily.*) We Jews do everything that is destined for us. Always with great reluctance, but we do it.

ZOAB: Come now, Sir. You are almost at the end of a slightly comic career. Can you still have faith in its seriousness?

SAMSON: We are always deadly serious when we make jokes.

ZOAB: If I may continue. You have been a criminal against us and by your own law owe us an equal return. By the calculation of our experts this has now been made.

SAMSON: (*Indignantly.*) But *I* have not serviced these foolish Philistine mothers.

ZOAB: That is a technical detail. In symbolic principle, you have now compensated us for our losses.

SAMSON: So what will you do next? Kill me a thousand times with the jawbone of an ass – symbolically, of course.

ZOAB: Fourteen. We might manage fourteen deaths. We are very skilful. Then of course there is castration.

SAMSON: What possible difference could that make to me?

ZOAB: But that we must reject on religious grounds. For us even the fertility of an enemy contains an element of the divine.

SAMSON: (*Breathes a sigh of relief.*) Strange how, though they grow increasingly less decorative and useful, one would rather keep the absurd regalia of one's manhood.

ZOAB: (*Thoughtfully.*) Our problem now is to discover a final solution to the Samson riddle.

SAMSON: Good. Perhaps Dagon works with Jahveh after all.

ZOAB: Possibly. Some argue that Jahveh is the best weapon we have against your superstitious tribesmen.

SAMSON: Well, certainly, He does make things difficult from time to time. But always according to a precise plan which He never discloses.

ZOAB: We believe that all gods, like the men who invent them, have their periods of disturbance. Recently your Jahveh seems as undecided as an adolescent girl.

SAMSON: But the more neurotic He becomes the more likely are we, His people, to regain that insane puritanism which in the past has made us heroic enough to defeat history.

ZOAB: The point is that your fate demonstrates clearly the frightful revenge Jahveh takes upon his erring favourites.

SAMSON: I wouldn't rely on fear of God to frighten the Jews, if I were you. They consider it their greatest virtue.

ZOAB: We, on the other hand, study these matters comparatively. We have established that your Jahveh is a desert wind-god glorified with the attributes of an Egyptian sun-god. The eyes of his heroes symbolize the heavenly orb. Their trailing hair and bristling beards, his virile rays.

SAMSON: Oh, when will you Gentiles realize that for the Jews there is no such thing as comparative theology? There is only our own, fixed immovably.

ZOAB: Nevertheless your ordinary people are not much different from our own. They depend on their land and their animals. Sympathetic magic is as irresistible to them as it is to our own peasants. When we put out your orbs, cut off your rays, we deprived your god of his potency so far as they are concerned. It is standard primitive logic.

SAMSON: In dealing with Jews, reason will get you nowhere.

ZOAB: I agree it is all very elementary, but our long practice in the business has shown us that it always goes down well with the general public. Your blindness has gelded your people.

SAMSON: So you use Samson's decline to make Jewish hopes a laughing stock in Gaza.

ZOAB: (*Sniggers.*) Well, you don't have to be Jewish to enjoy Jewish jokes.

SAMSON: Samson is a very tired joke. As my mother knows quite surely, I betrayed my destiny and was punished because I went with a Gentile girl. Now, please, I beg of you – do the same and let me rest.

ZOAB: Very well. (*He is about to start on the GIRL.*) You know it's strange that the special relationship you Jewish heroes are alleged to have with Jahveh, fails to restore you.

SAMSON: (*Sighs.*) True. No other people in history has managed to convince the world that it has a special relationship with a supreme being, and yet I feel so tired.

ZOAB: Wine and women restore man's spirit temporarily. This wine is especially strong. Why bother with your principles now? Take a glass.

SAMSON: I tried it once. It gives me heartburn.

ZOAB: Then take this woman. It may do you good.

SAMSON: My desire lies with my hair in a stuffed pillow under the head of a magnificent courtesan, who sleeps, I do not doubt, extremely well.

ZOAB: And you seriously maintain that all your fabulous strength supports her head?

SAMSON: I know it sounds as scientifically unlikely as the story of my birth. You know that fable of course.

ZOAB: Indeed. Like all Jewish heroes, you were conceived in extraordinary circumstances. These fables get more extreme every century. Eventually your people will produce a messianic hero out of a virgin by an insubstantial spirit.

SAMSON: (*Laughs shortly.*) Not even the Jews would swallow that. As for me, I was conceived in a field after a visitation from an angel who looked much like a randy Philistine squire out for an afternoon's ride.

ZOAB: It is possible. Our aristocracy have an insatiable fancy for Jewish girls.

SAMSON: If I am half a Philistine, how could I ever have been a perfect working instrument for Jahveh? You know how exclusive my God and people are.

ZOAB: Hmmmm. On the other hand, if you were half Philistine, Jahveh would know it, and if you were an imperfect instrument for Him, why should He use you for this obscure demonstration?

SAMSON: The demonstration has failed, has it not?

ZOAB: Most certainly.

SAMSON: And Jahveh always knows precisely what is going to happen?

ZOAB: So your priests maintain. Although to us it seems absurd to give one's god such total power.

SAMSON: It follows then that Jahveh does not want, and never has wanted, the Samson riddle to be unravelled. My story is yet another tragicomic Jewish tale with a sad ending. We have a lot of them.

ZOAB: Good. Perhaps I may summarize. Your theory is that Jahveh gave you this incredible strength knowing that you were an imperfect vessel to contain it and that the entire demonstration would be futile and end in ignominious failure.

SAMSON: (*Sighs.*) That's my God.

ZOAB: But what is the profit in this?

SAMSON: We are not a trading people like you Philistines. We are a simple, agricultural, territorially bound federation of tribes united by ten laws, which we break frequently, in the secure belief that we are the nominated protestants of an unseeable, unknowable, all-powerful God, who has reserved for us some special purpose in his quite understandable scheme of things.

ZOAB: From a merely human point of view, Samson, it is a most unsatisfactory position.

SAMSON: (*Wearily.*) As a mere human, Priest, I agree with you. Please now, I beg of you, service this child before she wakes and proclaims to the world my impotence.

(*ZOAB kneels down to the GIRL. She stirs. He looks up at SAMSON.*)

ZOAB: By the way. Does it occur to you –?

SAMSON: (*Irritably.*) What? What?

ZOAB: She –

SAMSON: This girl?

ZOAB: No – Delilah – this girl – woman – the Harlot herself.

SAMSON Well?

ZOAB: Make us their instruments.

SAMSON: They do. She did.

ZOAB: Well then, let me ask you one final question.

SAMSON: Ask for God's sake!

ZOAB: How could she do that against the intention of Jahveh?

SAMSON: Hmmmm. So?

ZOAB: Might she not be his instrument?

SAMSON: She might. And then?

ZOAB: *(Excited at his discovery.)* In which case is he not for us, for the Philistines – another guise of the Philistine god – is that not possible?

SAMSON: *(Wryly.)* Why not? Bless the name of the All-Possible and get on with the task in hand.

(ZOAB arranges the GIRL's legs.)

ZOAB: Yes, indeed – a most exciting thought. Thank you, sir, for a truly stimulating discussion. *(He sighs and get down to the sacred business in hand.)*

SCENE THREE: THE TEMPLE OF DAGON

(A highly dignified OLD PRIEST sits in a throne-like chair, and on a bench near him are two distinguished, middle-aged, executive PRIESTS. One of them reads from a tablet in his hand.)

2ND PRIEST: *(Reading.)* 'The convocation of Brides of Dagon – '

OLD PRIEST: *(Irritably.)* Does that mean the entire thousand stupid girls this Jewish eunuch is alleged to have fertilized?

2ND PRIEST: That is so, your Reverence. It should make a most impressive sight.

OLD PRIEST: But, surely, it isn't necessary to have all these caterwauling female idiots in the temple at the same time. You know what excesses of hysteria these nubile girls are prone to.

2ND PRIEST: We agree, Reverence. It is not a situation we look forward to, but we all feel it necessary to make a concrete demonstration of the extent to which the alleged power of this... *(He giggles.)* ...Jewish eunuch, as you so wittily put it, has been assimilated into our society.

1ST PRIEST: Our thinking, Reverence, is that the primitive strength so admired by our over-civilized people should be seen to re-enter our own socio-religious complex.

OLD PRIEST: (*Sighs.*) Our Order is becoming so sharp-minded it will cut us to pieces.

1ST PRIEST: (*Gently.*) We assure you, Reverence, that this entire occasion has been planned with great care.

2ND PRIEST: We are certain it will produce the desired results. (*He returns to the tablet in his hand and continues reading.*) So – 'The entire convocation of Brides of Dagon intone, "We have taken his strength into our wombs."'

OLD PRIEST: (*With distaste.*) Must we be so particular?

1ST PRIEST: (*Hurriedly.*) In any case, Reverence, we needn't bother you with the details. The ritual will conclude with the entrance of the Great Harlot herself.

2ND PRIEST: The Man of Dan, dressed as Our Lord Dagon, will be led forward to meet her. And then –

OLD PRIEST: Yes. Yes. Most theatrical, unspeakably vulgar, and certain to please the public.

1ST PRIEST: We expect at least two thousand witnesses of the ritual.

2ND PRIEST: Representatives of all our leading families will be there.

OLD PRIEST: It will be an occasion of unforgettable brilliance, a new ritual of historic significance. (*Sighs.*) Bless Dagon that my age and reverence save me from appearing on such occasions.

(*He signs the tablet. The light on him dim as the 1ST and 2ND PRIESTS walk forward.*)

2ND PRIEST: I thought he'd be much more trouble.

1ST PRIEST: He's very conservative. But he knows very well that the Order must develop with the times. It's just that he prefers to ignore the details.

2ND PRIEST: I must say I think it's going to be an absolutely divine spectacle. I mean when you think of what the protagonists have been to one another –

1ST PRIEST: I do think sometimes that you are altogether too involved in theatricals and tend to neglect the ideology.

2ND PRIEST: Well, after all, it is my job to arrange these things. I must say one gets very little credit in the Order for being creative. Everything is so political these days. Or even worse, financial.

1ST PRIEST: Well, dear friend, your creativity *is* somewhat expensive.

2ND PRIEST: I'm just so delighted that I haven't had to take some ghastly rich old bag for the Great Harlot. At least Delilah is excellent casting.

1ST PRIEST: (*Drily.*) And half a million in silver should at least cover the cost of your enchanting costumes.

SCENE FOUR: THE PRISON HOUSE IN GAZA

(*A light reveals a gigantic terrifying figure between two columns... When the lights are fully on, they reveal the 2ND PRIEST, assisted by THREE GIRLS costuming SAMSON as Dagon. From the temple above, sounds of a huge crowd.*)

2ND PRIEST: Just a moment, dear. (*He studies the costume.*) Yes. Not bad. Although I know we're going to have trouble with the fishtail. Where is the fishtail anyway?

GIRL: It's not finished yet.

2ND PRIEST: It's impossible. Even a professional would need some rehearsal with that contraption. And what have I got here? A blind amateur. (*Increasing sounds of crowd from above.*) Oh, listen to them! There just isn't time. They're going to have to manage without the fishtail. (*TWO PRIESTS enter hurriedly carrying a fishtail.*) No. No. No. It's quite useless now. There's no time to rehearse it. Take it back. (*The TWO PRIESTS run off with the fishtail.*) You two girls come with me. We'd better see how the Harlot's getting on. (*DELILAH enters dressed fantastically as the Great Harlot.*) Oh! I see you're getting on very well.

DELILAH: Leave us.

(*The masked head of SAMSON moves at the sound of her voice. The sound of the crowd from above grows louder.*)

2ND PRIEST: There really isn't very much time. We've got –

DELILAH: Leave us, I say.

2ND PRIEST: (*Petulantly.*) Oh! come on, girls.

(*He exits followed by two of the GIRLS. The third GIRL is adjusting SAMSON's costume with great absorption and does*

*not notice the others leave. DELILAH approaches and kicks the
GIRL.)*

DELILAH: (*With cold command.*) Get out, you little bitch!

GIRL: I – I am only doing my work, Lady.

DELILAH: (*Viciously.*) Go do it with some diseased beggar, you
gutter-scut!

(*SAMSON takes off his mask.*)

GIRL: (*Uncertainly.*) Shall I come back again later, Sir?

DELILAH: (*Quietly.*) Do so and I will have you split through
the middle.

GIRL: Oh!

(*She runs off terrified. As SAMSON walks forward from between
the two columns, DELILAH sees his blind face clearly for the first
time and is appalled.*)

DELILAH: Your eyes!

SAMSON: (*Mildly.*) You were hard on the girl. She's only
training to be another Delilah.

DELILAH: You stud! You Samson of little girls. Oh damn,
damn and damn you!

SAMSON: You have.

DELILAH: I had it in mind to say as I saw your face: 'Softly
awakes my heart.'

SAMSON: A trite phrase which will never serve to remember
us.

DELILAH: (*Intensely.*) I remember every colour in the multiple
rainbow of our love.

SAMSON: Oh, no!

DELILAH: (*Dramatically.*) The ever-changing memory obscures
the sun and illuminates the night, and there is no time left
for me but a time that is past.

SAMSON: An unearned income and a tragic affair have made
you into a bad lady-poet.

DELILAH: (*Indignantly.*) Do you remember nothing of our
love?

SAMSON: I remember something.

DELILAH: What? Tell me?

SAMSON: I remember a certain posture of your buttocks and
the whalebone resilience of your spine.

(*He stumbles as he tries again to move forward. DELILAH takes his arm.*)

DELILAH: Here.

SAMSON: Your hand.

DELILAH: You remember it?

SAMSON: Blindness exaggerates touch.

DELILAH: My touch was always sure upon you. Ah, that was love, love.

SAMSON: What had love to do with you except in a purely professional capacity?

DELILAH: Because I am no amateur, I take it seriously.

SAMSON: A million pieces of silver, they say.

DELILAH: Every woman longs for security.

SAMSON: Exactly. Love has a price.

DELILAH: Security is so costly.

SAMSON: Well, that's the price of love. I think that only seducers and ex-lovers ever talk of love.

DELILAH: What happened between us had the beauty of a great myth and will be remembered so.

SAMSON: Very likely. People only remember violent follies and immoderate revenges.

DELILAH: You did what few men have ever done.

SAMSON: I led men forward and found they were not following.

DELILAH: Oh, forget your unimportant military career. Your distinction is that you proved the existence of love for women.

SAMSON: So, I will comfort myself that a woman knows she has been truly loved.

DELILAH: What an unforgettable moment! As I loved you with one hand and cut your hair with the other, how hopeful I was that at last you had told me the truth, that destiny had chosen me to be the woman for whom a man would give all. If only I could make you understand what it means to a woman, who has all her life seen the promises of men explode like detumescent bubbles, to find the reality at last.

SAMSON: So, while I breathed out to you the secret of the world you were conducting some capricious female experiment.

DELILAH: I had to know. But, now, let all that be forgotten.

SAMSON: Not so easy. I have the darkness to remind me.

(*DELILAH stares into his face for a moment. She strokes his hair and face.*)

DELILAH: Your head is still magnificent but refined some how. I liked your hair short. It made you look boyish and vulnerable. Now it has grown again.

SAMSON: (*Sighs.*) Time to collect the dividend on your carefully invested million. Mock me.

DELILAH: (*Genuinely hurt.*) But I love you, my heart. I long for you, my lion. I ache and rave for you. My loins cry out for you. I am a vacuum without my Samson.

(*SAMSON pulls away from her.*)

SAMSON: This is too female to be believed.

(*DELILAH pursues him.*)

DELILAH: But that's what I am. Female is my nature.

SAMSON: Did you have some notion to get this vacuum which your nature abhors, filled?

DELILAH: Don't be bitter. It makes you crude.

SAMSON: Am I to grind daily for the Philistines and on the Sabbath tread Delilah's mill?

DELILAH: I don't wish to talk to you when you're in that mood.

SAMSON: Shall I be a bull six days a week and on the seventh your stallion?

DELILAH: Well, it's better than nothing. Listen to me, my dear. After the Great Harlot is married to the Lord Dagon in his Bull of the Sun manifestation –

SAMSON: What is this nonsense?

DELILAH: They're preparing you for the ceremony. I have bought the privilege of being the Great Harlot.

SAMSON: But what truly Great Harlot pays?

DELILAH: Be witty at my expense if you will. Pride is an impractical vanity women tolerate in men. I have none of it. So, listen. After this ritual marriage I can see no logical reason why we should not dwell together. We could make this Temple quite comfortable. (*There is increasing sound from the impatient crowd above.*) They're becoming impatient for us.

SAMSON: The building shakes under the feet of our wedding guests. (*He smiles.*) Who will ever believe that Delilah sacrificed her love for security and her fortune for marriage?

DELILAH: (*Impatiently.*) Any woman would. No more talk, love. Come, love me and then let us to our wedding.

SAMSON: I see how it is with women. They want everything.

DELILAH: That's not fair. It's simply that we need as much as we can get. (*Urgently.*) Come to me.
(*The ancient masonry of the temple groans under the weight of the crowd above.*)
Why do you wait?

SAMSON: I am studying the conclusion of my silly story. Is it that I, a general without an army, became an impotent fertility god in order to end a blind and therefore perfect husband?

DELILAH: The world is falling about us and you use the excuse of a simple accident to become an intellectual. It is something you were never very good at, brave heart. Come to me and I will cure you.
(*The sound of the building groaning. SAMSON still hesitates. DELILAH puts her arms about him.*)
Lie down. Be passive. We are part of it.

SAMSON: But what is it?

DELILAH: The riddle which is its own answer. Love me.
(*The sound of the groaning masonry becomes very loud.*)

SAMSON: What is that thunder? Is it an answer?

DELILAH: Forget the question. We only truly follow God's will when we forget about God.
(*There is a great sound of crying and shouting from above and tremendous thunderous sound as the temple collapses... In the sudden flashes of lightning-like strobe-lighting, the tableau of SAMSON and DELILAH together... There is, of course, no prop-masonry. The action is mimed. Blackout. Dead silence for five seconds.*)

SCENE FIVE: MANOAH'S HOUSE

(*MANOAH, the SCRIBE and SAMSON'S MOTHER.*)

MOTHER: (*Ecstatic.*) 'And Samson said unto the lad that held him by the hand…'

SCRIBE: (*Aside to MANOAH.*) He was found in her arms.

MANOAH: (*Aside.*) Shush!

MOTHER: 'He said, "Suffer me that I may feel the pillars whereupon the house standeth that I may lean upon them."'

SCRIBE: All the lords and the priestesses were on the roof. Above three thousand men and women. It was an old building. It collapsed. That's history.

MANOAH: Can history argue with people who have intimate contact with angels? Take it down.

MOTHER: 'And Samson called unto the Lord and said, "Oh Lord God, remember me I pray Thee and strengthen me I pray Thee. Only this once, oh God, that I may be at once avenged of the Philistines for my two eyes."'

SCRIBE: After this it will be war with the Philistines to the end of time. You know that, don't you?

MANOAH: Maybe that's what He wants.

MOTHER: 'And Samson said, "Let me die with the Philistines."'

SCRIBE: Shall I take it down?

MANOAH: (*Wearily.*) Take it down, take it down.

(*The SCRIBE writes as we fade out…*)

MOTHER: 'So the dead which he slew at his death were more than they which he slew in his life.' (*She sighs with deep satisfaction…*)

SCRIBE: It is written. Shall I read it back?

MANOAH: Read it back.

SCRIBE: (*Reads.*) 'The Story of Samson. And the children of Israel did evil again in the sight of the Lord; and the Lord delivered them into the hands of the Philistines forty years. And there was a certain man of Zorek, of the family of the Danites, whose name was Manoah; and his wife was barren…'

(*The curtain falls slowly.*
End of Play.)

THE HEBREW LESSON

Characters

JEW

MAN

TWO BLACK AND TANS

Voices

This play was first produced as a film entitled *The Irish Hebrew Lesson* in 1972, and won the Cork International Critics Prize. It was directed by Wolf Mankowitz and starred Milo O'Shea.

The Hebrew Lesson received its first stage-production at the Almost Free Theatre, London, in 1978, with the following company:

JEW, Leonard Fenton
MAN, Patrick Drury
1ST BLACK & TAN, Michael Low
2ND BLACK & TAN, Patrick Connor

Directed by Ed Berman

It was first produced in New York as *The Irish Hebrew Lesson* at the Colonnades Theatre Lab in 1980, directed by Michael Lessae.

The Hebrew Lesson

(*The large attic room of a decaying eighteenth-century house in Cork.
The room has been laid out roughly as the interior of a synagogue, with
a raised platform with a balustrade around its centre, chairs and benches
at present disarranged around it, and facing us with an embroidered
cloth hanging on it a large wardrobe, which is being used as the Ark
of the Law. An elderly JEW, bearded, wearing a skullcap and huge
praying-shawl, studies concentratedly at the lectern on the platform.
He might be praying, but actually he is learning the Irish for numbers
and certain essential phrases, translating them from his native Yiddish
into the English of the textbooks before him, and then into Irish. He has
lived in Cork for thirty years and has traces of an Irish accent upon his
Yiddish English.*
*From the streets outside, the sounds of firing, occasional shouts and boots
running over the cobbles, to all of which he does not react.*
The year: 1921. The time: very late on a mild Friday night.)

JEW: Einz, zwei, drei, fier, finf, sechs, sieben, ucht, nein, zehn.*
One, two, three, four, five, six, seven, eight, nine, ten. Aon,
dó, trí, ceathair, cúig, sé, seacht, ocht, naoi, deich. Penneh,
schilling, fund. Yedes schtick kost sechs penneh, odder
zwei far zehn penneh. A spezeeler preis. Pennies, shillings,
pounds. The price is six pennies each, or two for tenpence,
a special price. Pinginí, scilleaca, púint. Sé réal an ceann an
pragas nó dá ceann ar deic pingine, pragas specialta. Eer
kennt meer bezollen zwei penneh a vokh. I can collect two
pence vickler. Is féidir lom da pingin do bailiúgoluai. De
zeidene shull kost drei penneh. Siz gemucht von indishen
zeid. The silk scarf is threepence. It's an Indian silk scarf.
Ta tri pingin ar an scairf síodac. Is scairf indíuc síodac
é. Hoizen, was far a greis? Zocken, shvarts odder veiss,
emessdicker boimvol, a penneh mit a halleb yedes por.
Trousers, what size? Stockings, black or white, pure cotton,

---

* For pronunciation of Yiddish, Gaelic and Hebrew words, see Notes on
page 117.

three halfpence a pair. Brístí, cén tómas? Stocaí, dub nó bán fíor-cadás trí leitpingin peidre.

(*While he studies, a MAN has entered the open attic window silently, and stands frozen, a pistol in his hand trained upon the JEW. The sounds from the street are nearer and finally disturb him.*)

How can I study with such a ferkukte noise? Let innocent people sleep! Cossacks!

(*He gets up to close the window. As he does so the MAN draws back into the shadows.*)

(*Loudly.*) Chazerim! Pigs! Mumserim! Black and brown bastards! Bithiunaigh!

MAN: (*With a Cork accent.*) Quiet! Call them and you are a dead man.

JEW: Who said that?

(*The MAN emerges. He is very young, in nondescript clothes, his face pale, ascetic, that of a novitiate of religion or revolution.*)

MAN: Close the window and keep quiet.

JEW: That's a gun?

MAN: Close it!

(*The JEW shrugs, closes the window and draws a curtain.*)

JEW: You're a gunman.

MAN: I am.

JEW: You kill old men?

MAN: I do not.

JEW: So, put down the gun. It can go off.

MAN: (*Listening.*) Will you be quiet?

JEW: What should I do, sing?

MAN: I do not want to frighten you.

JEW: Who's frightened? I'm too old to be frightened. I've seen worse, Cossacks. The streets ran with blood.

(*The MAN comes into the area of light from another lamp on the platform.*)

Tsk-tsk. You're a young man, a boy almost.

MAN: Well, we're almost a young country. What is this place?

JEW: This is my stebl.

MAN What?

JEW: I am a Jew. This place is a synagogue, not the best in town, but at least I made it myself. A few of us like to keep the old style –

MAN: (*Suspicious.*) A Jew man? Here?

JEW: (*Shrugs.*) What can you do? We're a travelling people.

MAN: I know about you.

JEW: (*Curiously.*) What do you know? Did you see a Jew before?

MAN: One came to our market.

JEW: (*Interested.*) Oh yes? Where?

MAN: (*On guard.*) Why should you care?

JEW: Nothing, only if you met a market Jew I must know him.

MAN: I'm sure. You're a close lot.

JEW: What can you do? We're a small family.

(*The MAN laughs shortly with tense nervousness.*)

There's something funny?

MAN: Fat as a synagogue cat, my father used to say.

JEW: (*Puzzled.*) A synagogue cat?

MAN: (*Laughs.*) Yes.

JEW: Who keeps a cat in a synagogue?

MAN: Fat, you see, from the great feast of foreskins.

(*He laughs again. The JEW is a little put out.*)

JEW: Personally I don't think it's very funny, but laugh if you've got something to laugh about.

MAN: I'll stay here for a while.

JEW: Welcome. Take a seat.

(*He clears a space. The MAN crosses to the door, opens it carefully, looks out, and then closes it again.*)

Yes. I know all the markets and the pedlars, the Jewish ones. It was in the West, you say? Macroom?

MAN: Never mind.

JEW: Please yourself. You're one of those revolutionary boys?

MAN: No questions!

JEW: All right, you're a young angel of death. This is a holy house, so come in, angel. Oy, you look tired to death, angel.

MAN: (*Suspiciously.*) Were you talking Irish before?

JEW: Diá duit! Go mairir céad bliain is go raib fice mac agus míle muc agat.

MAN: What kind of greeting is that? Twenty sons and a thousand pigs!

JEW: (*Proudly.*) It's a little something I threw together myself. You think the customers will appreciate it? I need Irish for my business. I learnt: Diá duig. Slán leat. Slán agat. I sell goods by weekly payment. I'm a vickler. Ta fáilte rómat dom tig-se.

MAN: Gura mait agat. But twenty sons and a thousand pigs! There's nothing wrong with our old greetings. Céad mile fáilte águs bás don impíarialaí.

JEW: The first part I understand – one hundred and fifty thousand welcomes.

MAN: A hundred thousand.

JEW: All right. For you, a hundred thousand. What was the rest of it?

MAN: Death to the English!

JEW: A cholera on them, we used to say. Only then it was the Russian Empire. Where's all that gone? All these empires come down into the dust and then a little child walks on it.

MAN: Please God.

JEW: Now, that's a Jewish expression.

MAN: And Irish.

JEW: Why not? God is a marvellous linguist. You look pale. You look white as death. Poor young Angel of Death, sit down.

(*The MAN collapses into a chair, suddenly no longer on guard.*)

MAN: I've been running all night.

JEW: I remember the feeling.

MAN: Is there anything to eat here?

JEW: It's not a restaurant, but I'll find –

MAN: Or drink?

JEW: There's the wine for the Sabbath. (*He indicates the wine laid out for the Friday night ceremony.*) Take some.

MAN: Not strong drink. I'm a pioneer.

JEW: When about to die any man is a pioneer. Drink. It'll do you good. You can put the gun down.

(*The MAN puts the gun in his pocket, takes the bottle and drinks greedily from it. The JEW watches him for a moment, then looks at a table with the remains of a meal on it.*)

Good. I have a piece of gefilte fish still in the bowl I brought up for dinner. My daughter made it.

MAN: Fish?

JEW: Gefilte. Eat. It's Friday, isn't it?

MAN: That's fish in the Jewish?

JEW: That's the best fish in any language. Here! (*He offers the bowl and a spoon.*)

MAN: (*Doubtfully.*) Hmmmm?

JEW: Eat, eat.

MAN: (*Tastes it carefully.*) Hm!

JEW: It's good.

MAN: It's not so bad.

JEW: It's sustained the Jewish people like manna in a thousand desert lands.

(*The MAN eats with increasing appetite. The JEW watches him thoughtfully.*)

Did you kill somebody?

MAN: I told you, no questions.

JEW: I killed a man once.

MAN: You did?

JEW: It's not so difficult. But it was a pity. He was only a stupid peasant and drunk and poor. For him anti-Semitism was a kind of business, a pogrom was a chance to improve his standard of living. I didn't know I was hitting him so hard, with a poker it was. Still – what was the use of apologizing? His head was smashed in. After that I left. We came to Cork. That was in eighteen ninety-something. Now it's 1921. Time flies. You know something? I thought it was New York here, because the bastard in Lithuania who sold me the ticket told me it said New York!

(*The MAN has been eating the fish ravenously, not paying any attention to the JEW's conversation.*)

Just making polite conversation. The fish is good, eh?

(*The sound of a patrol car passing outside. The MAN starts.*)

MAN: I must go.

JEW: That's a good idea?

MAN: They'll search.

JEW: A Jewish house? What for? Downstairs is my daughter and her family, and downstairs again is the old iron, the silk scarves and the socks. In the backyard is a horse and cart and more old iron. Why should they search? Mind you, the horse is an Irishman. I call him Cuchulainn, because he's an old dog. (*He listens.*) They've gone.

MAN: (*Relaxes.*) Your pronunciation's not bad.

JEW: Thank you. Aach! At my age I must give myself lessons again. My family for a thousand years are learning new languages, but this is ridiculous. Tá trí pingin ar an scairf síodac.

MAN: Ceannóinn é ac níl trí pingin agam.

JEW: Now, just a minute. This is a good opportunity for a conversation lesson. Duitse pragas specíalta dá pingin ar an bfíor indíac síodac scairf.

MAN: That's very good, only you should say 'scairf indíac síodac'.

JEW: It's an impossible language. Thirty years I'm trying to learn.

MAN: Not at all. No more than yours.

JEW: Mine? Which mine? Yasik czary e ich kasaki? Vilst reden mummaloshen? What language is mine?

MAN: Say something in Jew language.

JEW: Vas fur a yolde!

MAN: What was that?

JEW: That's Yiddish. I'll read something in Hebrew.

MAN: What's the difference?

JEW: What's the difference between English and Irish? (*He opens a book and reads from a Psalm.*) 'Im ech-kachach Yurushalayim tish cach yimini.'

MAN: For God's sake!

JEW: (*Patiently.*) 'Im'.

MAN: 'Im' is butter.

JEW: In Irish it's butter. 'Ech-kachach' –

MAN: (*Curiously.*) 'Ech-kachach'.

JEW: (*Surprised.*) It's marvellous the way you make a 'ch'.

MAN: It's a sound only the English can't make. I have an old aunt who says the Irish are descended from the ten lost tribes.

JEW: I don't think so. They couldn't have got *so* lost.

MAN: (*Suspiciously.*) What do you mean?

JEW: Try again. 'Im ech'.

(*The MAN slowly repeats it after him, showing a quick ear for the language.*)

You've got a good ear.

MAN: What's it mean? For you a special price, twopence. (*He laughs.*)

JEW: (*Indignantly.*) Certainly not. No business in Hebrew. It's a holy language. It's for prayers, for psalms, for poetry, not for selling socks. Except in Palestine. They're growing trees there and picking oranges all in Hebrew. A group from my village went, some boys with long side curls and a few girls with red handkerchiefs round their hair. And now they are speaking Hebrew the whole time while they pick the oranges. That was before the war.

MAN: The German war?

JEW: The Japanese.

MAN: When was there a war with them?

JEW: Sometime. I forget.

MAN: Why didn't you go yourself?

JEW: I was a married man with a family and I sell socks. I don't grow oranges.

MAN: Oranges.

JEW: For me? What do I need it for? I'm a city man.

MAN: You city men are all alike.

(*Indistinct voices from the street below. The MAN starts.*)

What am I doing talking here? Thanks for your fish and your wine. I must be away.

(*From the street below voices are heard.*)

1ST VOICE: You two, try the alley!

2ND VOICE: Keep both ends of the street covered!

(*The JEW and the MAN look at one another in silence. The MAN takes out his gun.*)

MAN: Turn out the light and open the window.

JEW: Why draw attention?

MAN: Look, man, I shall have to shoot my way out. There's nothing else for it.

JEW: So, you'll get killed.

MAN: I'll not be the last.

JEW: You'll be the last and the first. Whoever destroys a single human life it's as if he has destroyed the whole world.

MAN: (*Impatiently.*) I've no time for talk. Put out the light!

JEW: Just a minute. (*He takes off his praying-shawl and puts it on the MAN.*)

MAN: What are you doing, for God's sake?

JEW: A minute, a minute! It makes you a better patriot to be dead? (*He opens a drawer and takes out a skullcap.*)

MAN: What are you thinking about? Look, they'll never take me for one of yours.

JEW: Try this one. It's nice, with a silk embroidery, from Palestine. (*He puts the skull-cap on the MAN's head.*)

MAN: Are you making a joke of me?

(*The JEW studies him carefully for a moment.*)

Finish now, will you? I look ridiculous.

(*Actually the MAN looks very Jewish, except for the gun in his hand.*)

JEW: There's something wrong. Of course –

(*He takes a prayer-book, puts it in the MAN's hand and takes the gun away.*)

Now, that's perfect. Maybe you even look Jewish. Just a minute! (*He turns the book round the right way.*) It reads from right to left.

MAN: Give it back here! (*He grabs his gun back.*)

JEW: As you like. But it spoils the whole effect.

MAN: I'll keep it hidden.

JEW: A gun under a praying-shawl! It's not nice.

MAN: (*Grimly.*) I'll try not to spoil it when I fire.

JEW: With God's help you won't fire.

MAN: You think God wants to save the lives of those bastards?

JEW: God wants us to study, that's what. Sit down! Read.

(*He shows him the place in the book.*)

MAN: Jesus! More lessons!

JEW: The same phrase. Try it. You never know when it'll come
   in useful.
   (*Sounds of men nearer outside.*)
MAN: (*Desperately.*) I must get out of here.
JEW: You'll never get away. Say again. 'Im ech-kachach
   Yurushalayim tish cach yimini. Tidbuck leshoni lechichi im
   lo ezerechi, im lo a'aleh et Yurushalayim ul rosh simchati.'
   Now try.
   (*He says the first phrase slowly in Hebrew again, and the MAN
   repeats it after him.*)
   Good, good. Again. 'Im ech-kachach Yurushalayim'.
MAN: 'Im ech-kachach Yurushalayim'.
   (*There is a noise on the stairs outside as heavy boots approach.
   The MAN starts up from his seat and reaches for his gun. The
   JEW puts his hand on his arm.*)
JEW: Quiet, quiet. Again. 'Im ech-kachach Yurushalayim'.
   (*The door is kicked open and TWO BLACK AND TANS enter.*)
1ST BLACK & TAN: What the hell's going on in here?
JEW: Good evening to you, officer, or, strictly speaking, good
   morning. In either case it's good to feel that a citizen's
   protected no matter what time of the day or night it is.
1ST BLACK & TAN: What's this, then? (*He looks round
   suspiciously.*)
JEW: This, officer, is a place of religious worship and
   instruction, a synagogue. It's not much but it's all we've
   got.
   (*The 2ND BLACK AND TAN is roughly searching for arms,
   making a mess in doing so.*)
2ND BLACK & TAN: Bloody Irish yid!
JEW: You put your finger on it instantly, Officer.
1ST BLACK & TAN: What are you doing up at this time of
   night?
JEW: We are religious men, Officer. What have we got to do?
   When we do not do business we study, and when we do
   not study we do business.
2ND BLACK & TAN: Bloody yids! Come on, Charlie, there's
   nothing here.
1ST BLACK & TAN: What's he, then?

2ND BLACK & TAN: Typical yid, ain't he?

JEW: A country man, just arrived. Doesn't speak a word of our beautiful English language. (*To MAN.*) 'Im ech-kachach Yurushalayim'. Right?

MAN: 'Im ech-kachach Yurushalayim'.

1ST BLACK & TAN: What did he say?

JEW: He made a blessing for you. He's a religious boy.

2ND BLACK & TAN: Bugger his blessing! Let's get on, Charlie.

1ST BLACK & TAN: Just a minute. Have a look around. (*Pointedly.*) See if there's anything suspicious we ought to take away with us. Right?

2ND BLACK & TAN: (*Delighted.*) That's right. These yids have got all sorts of very suspicious gold candlesticks and all that kind of clobber, 'aven't they?

JEW: You are welcome to search. Any gold candlesticks we have got we are pleased to contribute to your noble cause. These are brass. (*He looks to the MAN and nods.*)

MAN: Im ech-kachach Yurushalayim.

(*The 2ND BLACK AND TAN examines the brass sticks and throws them down disgustedly.*)

JEW: My friend agrees. He says help yourself to the gold candlesticks.

(*The 2ND BLACK AND TAN continues opening cupboards, making a mess, throwing holy books and praying-shawls out disgustedly. The MAN is barely able to suppress his fury at this. The JEW again restrains him with a look.*)

Im ech-kachach Yurushalayim.

1ST BLACK & TAN: Fat as a synagogue cat. Look at him!

JEW: Chup a cholera, du mumserim! Bless you, Sir!

1ST BLACK & TAN: Bloody unholy gabble! Come on, Tom, let's get out of this Jew shit-house!

(*A voice from below is heard.*)

VOICE: What the bloody hell are you two doing up there? Having an orgy?

1ST BLACK & TAN: Nothing up here, Sergeant-Major. Coming right down, sir. Come on, Tom, for Christ's sake!

2ND BLACK & TAN: Might as well take this.

(*He picks up the bottle of wine, takes a drag and spits it out, spraying the JEW and the books.*)

Bleedin' hell. What kind of Jew piss is that?

(*He tosses the bottle behind disgustedly as they both exit. The JEW listens a moment to the sound of the descending footsteps, wiping off the wine from his face.*)

MAN: Bastards.

JEW: At least they appreciate the jokes your father taught you.

(*The JEW closes the door and sets about picking up the books and refolding the shawls. Each book as he lifts, he touches briefly with his lips, and wipes.*)

MAN: (*With self-disgust.*) The dirty, filthy, stinking, murdering bastards! I should have shot them down.

(*He throws the cap and the shawl off furiously. The JEW calmly continues to tidy up.*)

JEW: Sure. We would all be meat in the gutter by now. Perfect dignity is a dead man?

MAN: We're different from you. We fight for our dignity.

JEW: (*Shrugs.*) Please yourself. But do me a favour, please, don't fight for mine. I prefer to live and remember.

MAN: I am prepared to die for my cause.

JEW: Well, that's brave. But from my life I can tell you that it's harder to live.

MAN: What's the use of talking? I must get on.

JEW: Anyway, don't feel too bad about it. You can die another night, if you insist.

(*A WOMAN'S VOICE is heard from below.*)

WOMAN'S VOICE: Father, are you all right?

JEW: (*Calls.*) I am all right. The lesson is going perfectly. (*To MAN.*) Better wait another hour or two. The curfew will be over.

MAN: (*Uncomfortable.*) I must thank you.

JEW: You already thanked me.

MAN: It's an odd thing to find one of you on our side

JEW: The hunted are all on the same side.

MAN: (*Hesitantly.*) Maybe I should tell you –

JEW: (*Quickly.*) Don't tell me anything.

MAN: You're right.

(*There is the sound from the street below of the soldiers and the patrol cars leaving. The MAN and the JEW listen. Then there is a moment of absolute quiet.*)

They won't come back this way now.

JEW: Maybe.

MAN: I'll be going on, then.

JEW: I expect so.

(*The MAN, about to leave, hesitates and turns.*)

MAN: I don't understand you people. Weren't you even angry when they threw your holy books down?

JEW: Books are just books, only the words are holy. You remember? 'Im ech-kachach Yurushalayim'.

MAN: 'Im ech-kachach Yurushalayim'.

JEW: That's very good. Your accent isn't bad at all.

MAN: What does it mean?

JEW: 'If I forget thee, O Jerusalem, may my right hand lose its cunning. May my tongue cleave to the roof of my mouth if I forget thee, Jerusalem.'

MAN: I know the passage well. It's in our Bible.

JEW: I'm glad to hear it. So, be careful.

MAN: I will.

JEW: Remember, God loves a live man just as much as a dead boy.

MAN: (*Smiles.*) I'll remember.

JEW: Good boy. Maybe you'll be President one day. Lech leshalom.

MAN: Imig i síocán.

(*The MAN exits by the door. The JEW looks after him for a moment, then crosses to the lectern, humming to himself, and continues his lesson from a small book.*)

JEW: Sé sé pingin an ceann an pragas. The day is not good. Níl an lá go mair. The morning is not nice. Níl an maidin go deas. The night is very long. Tá an oice ana fada. Aaah! (*He sighs deeply, suddenly very tired, and the curtain descends as he closes his eyes and rests his head on the lectern.*)

NOTES AND PRONUNCIATION

(The sound represented by 'kh' is the same as 'ch' in the Scottish 'loch' or German 'nicht'.)

Page 105 (*Yiddish.*) Eynss, tzvy, dry, fear, fineff, zecks, sibben, ukht, nyn, tzen. Penneh, shilling, foond. Yédess shtick kost secks penneh, odder tzvy far tzen penneh. A spétzee'éller pryce. Eer kent mere betsóllen zvy penneh a vokh. Duh zýdenne shull kost dry penneh. Siz gemúkht fon índishen zyde. Hoitzen, voss far a gryce? Zócken, shvarts odder vyss, eméssdicker boímvoll, a penneh mit a hálleb yédess por.

(*Gaelic.*) Ay-un, dhough, tree, káhir, cóo-ig, shay, shakht, okht, na-ay, deh. Pínginee, shíllukha, póo-int. Shay ráyul un kay-ann un price, noo gaw kháy-ann er deh-bíngineh, price spesheeúlta. Is fáydir lum gaw fingin duh varlóo golóo-a. Tam tree píngin er un skayrf shée-dukh. Is skayrf indéeukh shée-dukh aye...

Page 106 ...Bréeshtée, kane toce? Stuckée, duv noo bawn, feer shá-dows tree le fíngin un pýre-eh.

'ferkukte': (farkúkte) – shitty
'chazerim': (khazérim) – pigs
'mumserim': (mumzérim) – bastards
'bithiunaigh': (bihóonikh) – bastards
'stebl': (shteeble) – prayer room (literally: 'little room')

Page 108 'Diá duit! Go mairir céad bliain is go raib fice mac agus míle muc agat': (dee-á guít, guh marir káy-ud bleen is guh rev fíheh mac óggus méela muk oggút) – Good day! May you live for a hundred years and have twenty sons and a thousand pigs

'Diá duig. Slán leat. Slán agat': (dee-á guit, slawn lath, slawn oggut) – Good morning, goodbye, farewell

'Ta fáilte rómat dom tig-se': (taw fóyle-he róte dum híshe) – You are welcome to my house

'Gura mait agat': (górra mah óggut) – Thank you

'Céad mile fáilte águs bás don impíaríalai': (káyud méela fóyle-he óggus bowss dun impéeree-ulee) – A hundred thousand welcomes and death to the imperialist

Page 109 'gefilte fish': (gefilter fish) – stuffed carp or boiled, seasoned fish cakes

Page 110 'Cuchulainn': (coo-khóolin) – literally 'Culan's Hound'. One of the great heroes of Irish mythology, Cuchulainn when a child killed the watchdog of the Smith Culan, but made amends by undertaking to guard the house in the dog's place.

'Tá trí pingin ar an scairf síodac': (thaw tree fíngin er un skáy-arf shéedukh) – The silk scarf is threepence

'Ceannóinn é ac níl trí pingin agam': (kháyán-ówing aye akh neel tree fíngin oggum) – I'd buy it only I've not got threepence

'Duitse pragas specíalta dá pingin ar an bfíor indíac síodac scairf': (duít-she price speshiálta gaw fíngin er un vée-ur indéeukh shéedukh scayrf) – For you a special price, twopence for the pure Indian silk scarf

'Yasik czary e ich kasaki': (yásick kazáree ee eech kasáki) – The language of the tsars and their Cossacks

'Vilst reden mummaloshen?': (vilst rayden múmmaloshen) – Do you want to speak Yiddish?

Vas fur a yolde (vass fur a yolder) – what an idiot

'Im ech-kachach Yurushalayim tish cach yimini': (eem ésh-kakhékh yeróoshalayim tíshkukh yeméenee) – If I forsake thee, O Jerusalem, may my right hand lose its cunning (*Psalm 137*)

Page 113 'Tidbuck leshoni lechichi im lo ezerechi, im lo a'aleh et Yurushalayim ul rosh simchati': (tídbuck leshónee lekhéekee im lo ezkerékhee, im lo a'aléh et yeróoshalayim ull rosh simkhátee) – May my tongue cleave to the roof of my mouth if I forget thee, O Jerusalem (*Psalm 137*)

Page 114 'Chup a cholera, du mumserim': (khup a kholléra, doo mumzérim) – Catch cholera, you bastards

Page 116 'Imig i síocán': (ímig ee héekháwn) – Go in peace

'Se sé pingin an ceann an pragas' (shay shay fíngin un káyun un price) – The price is sixpence each

'Níl an lá go mair': (neel un law guh mah-uh) – The day is not good

'Níl an maidin go deas': (neel un vádin guh dass) – The morning is not nice

'Tá an oice ana fada': (thaw un ée-heh ánna ádda) – The night is very long

THE BESPOKE OVERCOAT

AUTHOR'S NOTE

Love is a luxury which very poor people can afford, and *The Bespoke Overcoat* is a story of this love. It is not a love which conquers all. Fender does not get enough food or a tailor-made overcoat, in this life. In life he does not find satisfaction, except insofar as he is able to accept with humour and humility the deprivations forced upon him. It is because this humour and humility is shared with his friend that Fender, in spite of everything, would prefer to go on living. To prefer to go on living is to love in the context of this story, and because this is loving at its most deprived the story is a sad one.

In producing *The Bespoke Overcoat* that remarkable artist Alec Clunes concentrated entirely upon this feeling which, by its intensity, animates a piece which is not well-constructed. The story was written without any directions for staging or the production of effects. The only stage, the only effects, the only theatre I had in mind were in the heart of a drunken tailor. There was no indication of time past or time present, because a twinge of conscience lasts a moment or a lifetime, and *The Bespoke Overcoat* is about the unreasonable conscience felt by the poor who love the poorer with a love which conquers nothing.

So Alec Clunes' production, which was, in effect, the writing of the play for the practical stage, dispensed with sets, used the barest properties, used darkness broken by three constantly moving areas of light, to tell a simple story with great simplicity. He realized that Fender was not a ghost and that this story was not a ghost story; he understood that *The Bespoke Overcoat* was a sustained, typically over-long Jewish joke – than which there is no sadder and no funnier story. And I am deeply grateful to him for having understood so much, for having made it available to other people, and for having taught me in the process, as he has taught so many other artists, something of the meaning of theatre.

Characters

MORRY, a tailor

FENDER, a warehouse clerk

RANTING, his employer

CLERK

The Bespoke Overcoat was first performed in 1953 at the Arts Theatre, London, with the following company:

MORRY, David Kossof
FENDER, Alfie Bass
RANTING, Harold Kasket
CLERK, Oscar Quitak

Directed by Alec Clunes

The Bespoke Overcoat

(*The action of the play is distributed among three separate areas permanently set and used in turn.*

Area 'A', midstage right, is RANTING's warehouse, which consists of a sizeable table, placed obliquely, with a chair or stool left and to the upstage end of it. Upstage of the table and rather behind it, a large rack supports a selection of overcoats on hangers.

Area 'B' is downstage centre and has no furnishing.

Area 'C', midstage left, is MORRY's room, which consists of a mattress lying obliquely on the floor, and beside it, right, at the upstage end, a chair.

These three areas are encompassed by a black surround with entrances down right, down left, and up centre. During the entire play, these are in total darkness, as are any two of the acting areas not being used. Throughout, the stage directions will be related to the three areas described.)

SCENE ONE

(*When the curtain rises MORRY is standing in area B with a navy blue overcoat over his arm. A barrel organ is playing, off, and fades out as the light at B fades in.*)

MORRY: Fender dead. That old man Fender dead. Funny thing. You're a good tailor, he used to say. You're a good tailor. Nu, you're a good tailor. Look around. I don't care where you look, he says, you are a number one tailor. Look at this coat, he says. What, that old coat? A coat must be twenty years old. Mind you, I can tell straight away by the cross stitch it's my coat. It's your coat, he shouts. You made it. Twenty-two years ago I come to you for a coat. This is him. I still got him. You got a good point. I tell him, I'm a good tailor. It's only the truth. I'm a good tailor. Straight away, I see I made a mistake. I fell in. How much, Fender says, will you take to mend a coat like this? I ask you. It's falling to pieces on his back. I told him straight, no nonsense. Look, Fender, I told him, I can run you up a pair of trousers from lining canvas you can walk up Saville

Road nobody can tell you from the Prince of Wales. But, Fender, do me a favour. Take the coat somewhere else. A new coat I can make, but the Union says no miracles. A rag, that's all. I got my clients to think about. Good afternoon. A lovely piece of worsted. Mind you, I got a suit length here: in a hundred year you wouldn't see nothing better. Clients. Fender dead. An old man. (*Turns upstage, still speaking.*) He sits in that stone-cold warehouse all day long. (*Turns head round to audience.*) Who could mend such a coat? (*Moves slowly upstage to centre exit.*) That's enough. (*Light starts to fade.*) Leave me alone. All this nagging, nagging. (*He has gone, and so has the light.*)

SCENE TWO

(*As the light fades in on C, sitting cross-legged and hunched on MORRY's mattress is FENDER. He rubs his hands.*)

FENDER: Oy. How that Morry can thread a needle in this cold, I don't know. Such a cold.

MORRY: (*Entering upstage centre.*) I got trouble of my own. After all, I'm in Bond Street? I'm a merchant prince? I'm not even a limited company.

FENDER: I thought you was a limited company.

MORRY: (*Turning.*) Me? Never. What do I want with shares and directors? So – what can I do for you? It's late, but…

FENDER: To be Managing Director is not a nice thing? You got no ambition? Terrible cold in here. My old governor – Managing Director three companies. Chairman – six companies. But what a man! (*Rises.*) Look, Morry. I still got no overcoat. Put on the gas-ring.

MORRY: Fender! You ain't dead?

FENDER: Sure I'm dead. Would I sit up half the night in the freezing cold if I wasn't dead? I can tell you, I won't be sorry to get back. They got central heating, constant hot water, room service. And the food – as much as you like. Kosher, of course.

MORRY: (*Holding his head.*) I won't touch the rotten brandy.

FENDER: Drinks? You can have what you like, any time, day or night, on the house.

MORRY: Go on. So tell me, Fender. Is it really you?

FENDER: (*Holding out his hand.*) Feel my hand. Feel.

MORRY: (*Taking his hand.*) Believe me, you are cold. That lousy brandy. It kills you. (*Sneezes.*)

FENDER: (*Sitting on chair.*) Gesundheit.

MORRY: Thank you.

FENDER: All I want is to get back. Listen, Morry. You know the first person I met down there?

MORRY: Down there?

FENDER: I tell you, Morry, a secret: everybody goes down there. You know who I met? Lennie.

MORRY: Lennie from Fournier Street?

FENDER: Who else? He's doing the same job. And *what* herrings! I tell you, Morry, I won't be sorry to get back.

MORRY: (*Kneeling on mattress.*) Fender! You don't hold that overcoat against me, do you Fender? Believe me, if I had known you would catched a cold and died I would give you my own coat.

FENDER: That blankety coat. For that coat I'm here and not at the hotel. Look, Morry. I got nothing against you.

MORRY: (*Rising to one knee.*) You ain't going to haunt me, Fender? You wouldn't haunt an old friend?

FENDER: Don't talk silly, Morry. That haunting is a special job. They don't give it to new residents. For haunting you get a commission.

MORRY: (*Rising and moving behind FENDER. Crossing arms.*) So listen, Fender. It goes without saying I am pleased to see you. I'm glad you enjoy being dead. But you won't think I am rude, if I ask what you want of my life?

FENDER: I'll tell you. But first light that gas-ring so at least I won't freeze – listen to me – to death, I nearly said. You don't know, Morry, (*The light begins to fade.*) what sort of life it was at that Ranting clothing company. No wonder I didn't lose any sleep about dying… (*The light has gone.*)

SCENE THREE

(*The light fades in on A. FENDER is sitting on the stool with his notebook and pencil on the table in front of him. The conversation continues from the previous scene.*)

FENDER: After that warehouse for forty-three years, any change would be a pleasure. Forty-three years a shipping clerk.

MORRY: (*Off.*) So long?

FENDER: Forty-three years next Purim, if I didn't die before. (*RANTING enters down right carrying a board with lists.*)

RANTING: (*To behind desk.*) And sixty gross denim trousers.

FENDER: (*Writing.*) Sixty gross denim trousers.

RANTING: And forty gross cellaloid collars.

FENDER: Cellaloid collars. Forty gross cellaloid.

RANTING: (*Tapping with pencil, impatiently.*) Cellaloid makes with a C, no S.

FENDER: And what more?

RANTING: Eleven dozen raincoats, Prussian collar.

FENDER: Eleven dozen raincoats.

RANTING: Prussian collar.

FENDER: You know something, Mr Ranting? It's cold in this warehouse. I said it's cold, Mr Ranting. I feel the cold something terrible.

RANTING: Fender, I don't think you enjoy your work like in the olden days. (*Sits on table, head turned half downstage towards FENDER.*)

FENDER: What an idea! I enjoy my work? Certainly I enjoy. I feel the cold, that's all.

RANTING: Naturally, you are getting on. The work is hard. Nobody is as young as he used to be.

FENDER: What are you talking, Mr Ranting? Nobody is as young as he used to be? And how could he?

RANTING: I am saying, Fender, an old man is an old man.

FENDER: (*Rises.*) Certainly. Of course. An old man is an old man. Mr Ranting, I tell you something: my father, when he was seventy – no, over seventy – he can bend a horseshoe straight with his bare hands. And even he felt the cold.

RANTING: (*Getting off table.*) All I am saying, Fender, is stop driving me mad with your crying 'it's so cold, it's so cold'. Get a new overcoat; you won't feel it.

FENDER: I make an arrangement with you, Mr Ranting. I'll take one of the overcoats, the big ones with the sheepskin lining, and every week from my wages take off a certain sum. (*Holds out his hands.*) A proposition, Mr Ranting?

RANTING: One of them coats, Fender? Leave me alone.
(*FENDER moves as if to speak.*)
Hup! A coat like this is worth twenty pound anybody's money. What do you make? With all due respect, Fender, what do you make? You won't live so long to pay off such a coat.

FENDER: (*Sitting on stool, again.*) That's true. So what can you do?

RANTING: (*Reading from list.*) Seventeen dozen pair shooting breeches.

FENDER: (*Writing.*) Seventeen dozen pair breeches.

RANTING: Shooting.

FENDER: Shooting, shooting. (*Indicates the entry in his book.*)

RANTING (*In disgust.*) Ah! (*Exit down right.*)

FENDER: (*Rising and taking off his coat.*) Maybe Morry can mend the old coat again.
(*Cross fade lights from A to C.*)
After all he's a good tailor. (*Turns upstage as the light goes.*)

SCENE FOUR

(*As the light fades in on C FENDER is standing upstage of mattress. MORRY enters down left.*)

MORRY: Look, Fender, look. The seams is all rotten. Look, the lining is like ribbons. Look, the material is threadbare.

FENDER: A tailor like you, Morry, to make such a fuss. You should be ashamed.

MORRY: (*Sitting on chair.*) The padding is like an old horse blanket.

FENDER: Who asks for new padding? Only make the coat good. Who cares about the padding, so long as the coat is warm?

MORRY: It can't be done.

FENDER: Don't make jokes, Morry.

MORRY: If I say it can't be done, it can't be done.

FENDER: So, all right, charge a little more.

MORRY: Charge! What does charge matter? It can't be done.

FENDER: Why are you so hard for, Morry? After all, you can patch with off cuts.

(*MORRY holds head in hands.*)

I am not asking, after all, for West End style; I should look so smart. I don't care how smart. Only mend the coat, Morry.

MORRY: Fender, listen to me, Fender. A good coat like I make has got twenty years wear. I double-stitch the seams with best thread, no rubbish. Every stitch I test, (*Bites imaginary thread.*) so it's good and strong. I use good material: crombie, tweed, what you like. The best. I use a lovely lining; someone else would make a wedding dress from it, such a lining I use.

FENDER: You use marvellous lining, Morry.

MORRY: I make the whole coat, the buttons' holes, the pockets, everything.

FENDER: Don't I tell everybody? Morry – a needle like Paganini. I tell everybody.

MORRY: I would make you such a coat for cost, Fender.

FENDER: How much costs such a coat?

MORRY: Three yards, say.

FENDER: Say two and a half

MORRY: And lining.

FENDER: Don't worry yourself with lining.

MORRY: I can make you a good coat for twelve pound.

FENDER: You can't mend the old coat?

MORRY: Please, Fender, do me a favour.

FENDER: I can ask? Twelve pound is money.

MORRY: (*Rises.*) Listen, Fender. I break my neck: ten pound for the coat. You got ten pound?

FENDER: I look like a banker? I can save ten pound.

MORRY: So.

FENDER: (*As he starts to put on his old coat.*) So. So I'm going to have made a bespoke overcoat.

MORRY: Bespoke is good.

FENDER: Certainly bespoke. You think I would wear Ranting's rubbish? (*Sits on chair.*)

MORRY: (*Moving downstage left and reaching offstage for patterns.*) What material you like?

FENDER: I can choose material?

MORRY: (*To FENDER with patterns.*) Here, patterns.

FENDER: The grey is not nice for me. The blue is better?

MORRY: (*Fingering the blue material.*) Blue is nice. You can wear blue for any occasion.

FENDER: Nigger brown is smart.

MORRY: For a young man.

FENDER: Black is always good.

MORRY: Black is good, but a nice, dark blue is nicer.

FENDER: (*Rising, and moving downstage of mattress.*) Believe me, Morry, I think you are right. The blue is good – and thick. What a material!

MORRY: (*Down to FENDER.*) I should say. So you can save ten pounds?

FENDER: Save? Sure I can save. An old man like me, if I got an overcoat, what do I need? (*Moving downstage centre to B.*) If I got a bespoke overcoat, what more can I need? (*Exit into darkness down right.*)

SCENE FIVE

(*MORRY takes out black bread etc. from his pocket and moves to his chair.*)

MORRY: With a piece of black bread and a herring you can't go wrong. You got in black bread vitamins, nutriment *and* a good flavour from herrings. In the old days, (*Sits.*) sometimes six clients a week, all wanting coats, suits, a spare pair of trousers, something. The trade is not good any more. Believe me, if I had a boy I wouldn't let him see a needle and thread. It's a thing of the past. Things are so bad now, you know what I'm doing? I'm making a ten-pound coat for Fender. For ten pounds, it's a wonderful coat. The material, the seams. No wind can blow through a coat like this. (*Rises and moves downstage a few paces.*) Let it blow as much as it likes. I read an interesting thing somewhere. When it's cold, it's not really cold. You are hot; that's why you feel the cold. Also you pull in your muscles. That's bad. Fender: his trouble is he's pulled his muscles so far in they won't pull any more. (*Moving down left to exit, as light fades.*) I was always interested in science things like this. (*Cross fade to B.*)

SCENE SIX

(*RANTING enters down right with a plate of chopped liver and a fork.*)

RANTING: The chopped liver is tukke good, Alf. You want some? Good boy. (*Stops down centre: B.*) Bring some more chopped liver, Maisie. So I was telling you, Alf: this exhibition they got such machines you wouldn't believe. They got a machine there – I'm not telling you a word of a lie, Alf – they got a machine can add up how much you made last year, take away your overheads, knock off your income tax, and show you if you got anything left. By my life. It has a dictation machine, a suspended filing system, a place special for telephone directories, and a permutator for working out football pools so they should win. And I worry myself to nothing, worrying, worrying the whole time over an old clerk's mistakes. What you say? Can a machine laugh like a man? Can it cry like a man? What difference? So long as a clerk clerks good, what difference he's laughing or crying? (*Exit down right in blackout as we hear FENDER laugh, off.*)

SCENE SEVEN

(*The light fades in on FENDER, laughing quietly, as he enters down right and moves to A, below table, with a half-eaten bagel wrapped in paper.*)

FENDER: A marvellous story, I must tell it to Morry. I enjoy a good laugh. (*He sighs and looks at the bagel.*) A bagel is enough. After all, bread and salt is food. It's the same dinner, only I leave out the soup. That woman, terrible, but what soup. I'm not saying it's not worth a sixpence. A bowl like that, where could you get it for sixpence? In a big restaurant they bring you half as much, and charge terrible prices. A woman cooks soup like that must make somebody a marvellous wife. Mind you, boss-eyed and what temper, a terrible woman. Still a bagel is plenty. Eat it slow, careful, every crumb does you good. Soup! Who wants soup? (*Moves upstage.*) When I get the coat, I put it on. I walk up to a table, (*Sits.*) I sit down in the overcoat, blue, nice: a bowl of soup, missus, and a bagel. (*Rises and moves a few paces downstage.*) Be careful! You want the soup should drop on this new overcoat – a bespoke overcoat – ruined. (*He laughs as, lifting the flap of his torn coat, his hand slips through a hole.*) I don't think I got room for these bits. No, I'm full up. I couldn't eat another thing, not even a fresh lutka or a piece of cheesecake. (*Turns to his accounts.*) Sixteen dozen flying jackets. (*Upstage to sit.*) With such jackets you can fly?

RANTING: (*Enters down right, moves behind table from which he brushes crumbs.*) How many times, Fender? Don't eat in the warehouse. It brings the mice. The mice eat the clothing.

FENDER: How many clothing can a little mouse eat?

RANTING: (*Reading.*) Twenty-eight gross denim trousers. (*Fade out.*)

SCENE EIGHT

(*Area C. Fade in on FENDER entering breathlessly up centre.*)

FENDER: (*Calls.*) Morry, I come to see how the coat is coming, Morry.

MORRY: (*Footsteps, off.*) The coat is all right.

FENDER: Which is the coat, Morry?

MORRY: (*Entering down left, with half-made coat.*) Here! Here!

FENDER: Should I try it on?

MORRY: (*Holding out coat.*) Try it on. Don't be shy. What's a matter with you? You're a film starlet, you got to have a changing room else you can't take off the old coat.

133

(*FENDER removes coat.*)

So. That's right. Take it off.

(*FENDER gives his coat to MORRY, who puts it on chair, and puts on the new coat.*)

FENDER: If I knew, I would put my other shirt on. You seen it, Morry? The drill shirt, with tabs on the shoulders, very smart.

MORRY: And why should you? Today is a bank holiday. Look. My own shirt. Everybody wears his old shirt for a working day. Nu. Try it.

FENDER: (*As MORRY fits the coat.*) In Clacton the sun is hot. This makes him the sun, you understand. What a hot! You got a nice deckchair, Mrs Felderman. I can see. A comfortable deckchair. Certainly a new overcoat – a bespoke overcoat. (*Lifts the left arm with sleeve in it.*) Suits me? Under the arms is a bit tight.

MORRY: (*Feeling armhole.*) It's fine. You got plenty room, look, look.

FENDER: A coat like this makes a difference.

MORRY: (*Kneeling in front to fit coat.*) Fender, you like the coat? What about a couple of pound on account? I got expenses. (*Rising.*) Can you manage a couple?

(*FENDER takes out purse, sorts out notes and silver, and hands them over with great dignity.*)

FENDER: Certainly. You know, Morry, twenty shillings, if you saved money like I do, thirty shillings, and didn't throw it away on that rotten brandy, thirty-five shillings, you would be a rich man. Forty shillings.

MORRY: And what would I do with my money?

FENDER: A question. What can you do with it?

MORRY: I can take an off-licence.

FENDER: An off-licence is a good idea. (*Taking off new coat.*)

MORRY: I use my knowledge. A special line in brandy. Old stuff – Napoleon – something good.

(*Takes overcoat from FENDER and hands him his old one.*)

FENDER: How can you know it's good?

MORRY: I try every bottle, personal. I put up a smart notice, 'Morry's Napoleon Brandy'; every bottle personal tasted. Thanks for the two pound. You can spare?

FENDER: Sure I can spare. The coat won't be long now, Morry?

MORRY: This week I make an exception. I have a drink tonight; that way tomorrow I take less.

FENDER: Tukke?

MORRY: Listen, Fender, drinking is by me not by you; it's my hobby so I shouldn't know? (*Exeunt. Cross fade to B.*)

SCENE NINE

(*When the lights go up on B, RANTING is strap-hanging downstage centre*)

RANTING: (*In a new coat.*) On the Central Line is always hot. You like the coat? Yesterday I picked it up. America style. (*Lurches.*) Sorry, Miss. Dear? I should say it's dear! You want me to wear one of me own coats? Twenty-five nicker – a pony, this coat – I beg your pardon. Knock off the booze and you'll be able to afford. My advice to you friend, is – knock off the demon drink.

(*He goes out down right Cross fade to C.*)

SCENE TEN

(*FENDER is asleep on MORRY's mattress, covered by the half-finished overcoat. MORRY enters drunkenly, upstage centre, singing and carrying a bottle.*)

MORRY: It says on the label extra special reserve, cognac Napoleon brandy, old special reserve. A brandy like this is a brandy like this. This. (*Drinks.*) A brandy. (*Turns to mattress.*) I got company? So late? (*Upstage to put bottle on chair.*) Hey, wake up. I got company. You sit here a minute. Don't go 'way. I'll come back. (*Kneeling upstage of mattress.*) Wake up, Fender, it's you? What an unexpected pleasure.

FENDER: (*Sitting up.*) I was having a dream. A flying overcoat and inside the pockets bowls of soup. And do you know, the soup never upset in the coat.

MORRY: I got here a brandy; you never drunk such a brandy in your life.

FENDER: (*Peering at the label.*) Special reserve. Must be good.

MORRY: Take a little drop. Go on. Take.

FENDER: (*Trying it.*) Ahh, like fire. (*Hands bottle back.*) A good one all right. Morry – Moishele.

MORRY: (*Holding out bottle in front of him.*) It's good brandy.

FENDER: I got bad news, Morry.

MORRY: Where can you find a brandy like this?

FENDER: That Ranting. He give me the sack.

MORRY: (*As he sits back on his heels and puts bottle on floor with a thud.*) He give you the sack?

FENDER: He give me the sack.

MORRY: After so long he give you the sack?

FENDER: He give me.

MORRY: He give it to *you*?

FENDER: The sack.

MORRY: Oy.

FENDER: I have with great regrets, Morry I must tell you, to cancel the coat. I came to tell you. Cancel the coat.

MORRY: (*Trying to give him the bottle.*) Take another drop brandy. Good for your cough.

FENDER: I don't fancy.

MORRY: Take. Don't be shy. Take.

(*FENDER drinks from bottle, and as he lifts his arm we see that the old coat is torn under the arm.*)

If I could mend that coat, Fender, I would mend it, I want you to know. I defy any master tailor to make that coat good.

FENDER: What can you do? It's just an old coat, that's all.

MORRY: (*Rises.*) You can't find the rest of the ten pounds? I'll finish the coat.

FENDER: How?

MORRY: (*Puts arm round FENDER and pats him on shoulder.*) With a needle. How else?

(*The lights slowly fade.*)

SCENE ELEVEN

FENDER: (*At B, downstage centre.*) I told him, polite, but strong. Mr Ranting, I been with this firm with your father and your uncle so many years. All this time I done the same job; nobody complains. Suddenly business is so bad you have to turn me off? Let him answer me that. No good. Excuses, anybody can find excuses. What I ask you, Mr Ranting, is, is it right? Let him answer me that. That's what I should have said. I should have told him off, big as he is. The governor, (*Turns upstage and spits.*) I used to give him a handkerchief he should wipe his nose. A little boy crying round the warehouse with his stockings down gives me the sack. Why didn't I tell him? Fender, he says, you got something put by, an insurance policy, something? I got something put by, don't worry. You got no family? Don't worry, I got plenty of family, I got friends. He worries about me. I even got a niece with a boarding-house in Clacton, and can she cook? Lovely weather the whole time. (*Turns upstage centre and then back to audience.*) Mind you, Morry is a good friend. In the morning I put on my new coat. I go to Ranting. I tell him. Give me that coat with the sheepskin. (*Coughs.*) Funny thing, a cough like this, comes right through you. Like a bowl of soup. It flies up through you like a flying jacket. There he goes.
(*He traces the path of the imaginary jacket round the theatre. It returns as the threatening celluloid collars. FENDER is dying.*) Seventeen dozen cellaloid collars, cellaloid makes with a C, no S – or S, no C. (*Weakly.*) Funny thing, I don't seem to know nothing any more. (*Sinks down as the lights slowly fade.*)

SCENE TWELVE

(*The lights fade in on area A as a CLERK, followed by RANTING, enters down right. RANTING goes upstage to behind table. CLERK sits at table with notebook and pencil.*)

RANTING: Thirty dozen pair shooting breeches.

CLERK: Thirty dozen pair shooting breeches.

RANTING: And a hundred dozen balaclava helmets.

(*MORRY enters upstage centre with finished overcoat over his arm.*)

MORRY: (*Coming to upstage of table.*) Mr Ranting. Excuse me, Mr Ranting.

RANTING: And sixty various drill jackets. Can I help you, Sir?

MORRY: I come for Fender. I finished him a coat.

RANTING: And two gross khaki drill shorts. He don't work here no more. I say work, but you should understand he was past it.

CLERK: Two gross shorts.

RANTING: Khaki drill.

CLERK: What?

MORRY: Khaki drill.

RANTING: Thank you. Fender lives by the arches in Flower and Dean Street. Or maybe with his niece at Clacton or somewhere. Pardon me. And twenty-eight pith helmets. (*Exit downstage right.*) Ah!

CLERK: Twenty-eight pith helmets. (*Rests his arms and head on table.*)

(*Cross fade A to C.*)

SCENE THIRTEEN

(*Area C, continuing as from SCENE TWO; MORRY is upstage of mattress, level with FENDER, who sits in chair.*)

MORRY: So I go to your lodging. I knock on the door. No answer. I knock again. An old woman comes. She's a bit deaf.

FENDER: She's stone deaf. A bit, he says.

MORRY: I shout in her ear, where is Fender? Fender – Fender! Where should he be? He's dead. He didn't have my age, but he's dead. You can knock me over with a feather bed.

FENDER: She got her head screwed on, the old girl. I was dead all right. Mind you, she makes out she's older than she is. I don't like that sort of thing.

MORRY: But so sudden.

FENDER: (*Rising and crossing in front of MORRY.*) Listen, Morry. You die when you are ready? You die when you have to, that's all. Still, I haven't done so bad. I can't complain. If only I kept my mouth shut I would be all right.

MORRY: I made the coat as quick as I can, Fender. (*Sits in chair.*)

FENDER: Look, Morry, I got nothing against you. You behave like a perfect gentleman. I told everybody at the hotel. Morry's a wonderful tailor. You think you look smart? Wait until Morry gets here. No. It was that Ranting. You see, Morry, I didn't take too long dying, but the whilst I am screaming and cursing, using terrible language, all against that Ranting. And when I get down there, it must have been on my mind. So the first couple of weeks, I am stopping the porter, the commissionaire, the chambermaids, even the guests, telling them about the overcoat. At last, they can't stand it any more. The manager sends for me. Fender, he says, you like the hotel? It's a wonderful hotel, I tell him. Everything of the best. I am very satisfied. Look, Fender, he says, I am very glad if you are comfortable, but I have to tell you everyone has a headache with your overcoat. Do me a favour: go down to the cloakroom, pick yourself any coat. Thank you, I tell him. It's not the same. I can see he is upset. I can't have the place turned upside down, he says. (*Pointing upwards.*) You'll have to go back for a while. When you get it, (*Points downwards.*) come back. It's on my mind, I told him. Next thing I know, I'm here. And here I am.

MORRY: (*Half rises.*) And I got your overcoat all wrapped up ready, Fender. Take it and good luck to you.

FENDER: (*Moving downstage, level with bottom of mattress.*) It's no good, Morry. It wouldn't make me happy. Somehow, I got to have that sheepskin coat from Ranting. I am not saying your coat isn't wonderful. It is. But I must have from Ranting a coat. I give him forty-three years nearly. He must give me a coat.

MORRY: (*Moving down to FENDER with bottle.*) You know what?

FENDER: What?

MORRY: We go to Ranting's and take the coat. That's what. (*Drinks.*)

139

FENDER: (*As MORRY offers him the bottle.*) Not a bad idea. (*Drinks and returns bottle. Exeunt downstage left with MORRY's arm round FENDER. Cross fade to A.*)

SCENE FOURTEEN

(*As the light fades in on A, RANTING enters from upstage centre, singing. The CLERK is seated at the table, writing in his notebook.*)

RANTING: That book you been making up for the past hour, what's the matter, you can't read?

CLERK: The old clerk had his own way of doing things. It takes a little while to work out. But I mastered it.

RANTING: (*Taking hat off.*) You got your head screwed on right. You go to the dog tracks in the evening?

CLERK: Not for me, Mr Ranting.

RANTING: Horses?

CLERK: No horses, neither.

RANTING: You must spiel something. Poker, shemmy?

CLERK: (*Rising and moving behind his stool.*) I'm developing myself, Mr Ranting.

RANTING: Something new?

CLERK: The human frame has nine hundred seventy-six individual muscles, each of whom can be developed up to peak power, give proper exercises and consideration.

RANTING: Nearly a thousand? So many?

CLERK: It has been proved by the best efficiency authorities that each of these muscular resources is vital to one. And what do we do? You sit cramped – like this. The muscles get slack and useless. You stand like this. The muscles suffer.

RANTING: Sit and stand you can't avoid.

CLERK: (*Taking off his overalls.*) Look at this, Mr Ranting. (*Rolls up sleeve and demonstrates muscle.*)

RANTING: Marvellous. Like Kid Berg. You should be a boxer.

CLERK: Worse thing you can do for the muscles, boxing. Fatal to the muscle tone.

RANTING: So what can you do with all them muscles?

140

CLERK: So far, I still have four hundred and eighty-nine
    muscles undeveloped.

RANTING: And then?

CLERK: I hope to stand as Mr Universe.

RANTING: A meshuggus. Put back the coat.

CLERK: (*Restoring coat and moving downstage right.*) When I get
    these pecs up I'll take my first competition.

RANTING: Local? (*Picks up CLERK's notebook.*)

CLERK: Down at the Roxy.

RANTING: Maybe I'll come.

CLERK: You'll enjoy it, Mr Ranting. The body beautiful.

RANTING: So I'll enjoy it. The whilst Mr Universe, go shut the
    door. (*Pushes CLERK out down right and follows him.*)

SCENE FIFTEEN

(*MORRY and FENDER enter down left and move towards area
B where the light now is. They are arm-in-arm, singing and
stumbling. MORRY carries an empty beer crate.*)

MORRY: In your position, Fender, it's not professional to
    drink so much at once.

FENDER: You know I met Lennie?

MORRY: You were saying before. How is he doing?

FENDER: Very nice. They let him open a little stall outside the
    hotel, on the promenade. You can get any kind of herring
    from him.

MORRY: (*Puts crate down and stands on it.*) I get in the window
    and give you a lift up. Just a minute. (*Gets down.*) See if you
    can walk through the wall.

FENDER: (*Crossing to right of MORRY; pauses.*) Don't talk silly,
    Morry.

MORRY: If you're a ghost you can walk through walls. And if
    you're not a ghost at least it's scientific experiment.

FENDER: It's true. I'll try. (*He tries.*) I feel silly. Get through
    the window, Morry. Just a minute. (*Takes key from pocket.*)
    A solution. I'll go round and open the door. (*Exit down
    right.*)

MORRY: (*Gets on crate and tries to open window.*) I can give myself a stricture with this. Shift, you – it don't budge. Get up.

FENDER: (*Off.*) I done it. Come round. It's cold in here.

MORRY: (*Getting off crate and picking it up.*) It would be nice if he walked through the wall, like I told him. (*Moving right.*) I even got to tell him how to be a ghost proper. (*Exit down right. Blackout.*)

SCENE SIXTEEN

(*Area A. FENDER enters upstage centre with a torch and crosses right to switch on imaginary light.*)

FENDER: It's easy. You should try. I'll just switch on the light.

MORRY: (*Follows him in as the lights come on.*) Right. Now, let's see. You remember where the coat is?

FENDER: (*Moving upstage of stool.*) Wait a minute. Trousers over there. Jackets here. (*Turns to audience.*) Would you believe it? I haven't been away five minutes and they shift the jackets.

MORRY: (*Moving to upstage of coat rack.*) Here are the coats. What about this? What a terrible cut. This one?

FENDER: (*Taking his old coat off and examining coat rack.*) Not for me.

MORRY: The blue is nice.

FENDER: No.

MORRY: It's a silk lining. A good lining.

FENDER: For what?

MORRY: This?

FENDER: Too short. (*Takes out coat with sheepskin lining.*) Ah! Ah! This is different. This I'll take.

MORRY: It's a nice weight, Fender, (*Helping him on with it.*) but the workmanship. Not nice.

FENDER: (*Moving downstage centre.*) How many times do I have to tell you, Morry? It's not personal. Only I must have one of Ranting's coats. That's all. He owes me.

(*On these lines FENDER becomes, it seems to us and to MORRY, less mobile, more like a dead man.*)

MORRY: (*Moving downstage to right of FENDER.*) Terrible cold in here. So. Can you go?

FENDER: I can go.

MORRY: My work is better.

FENDER: Certainly your work is better.

MORRY: So now you're all right, heh?

FENDER: I feel all right.

MORRY: Fender, you know something. (*Hesitates.*) This brandy is good.

FENDER: So – thank you, Morry.

MORRY: So, Fender, you're going now? You'll go back to the hotel?

FENDER: (*Turning upstage.*) Where else have I got to go to?

MORRY: Fenderler – you should give to Lennie my best regards.

FENDER: (*Turning back to MORRY.*) He's selling herrings like hot cakes, all day long. (*Moves upstage.*) He'll be pleased. A long life to you, Morry. Pray for me. (*His voice fades on this line and he has gone.*)

MORRY: (*Calls after him.*) May you come to your place in peace, Fender. (*Putting his hat on to pray.*) Yiskadal, veyiskaddish, ...

(*The Hebrew prayer for the dead is broken by barrel-organ music, off, as MORRY's head sinks upon his chest.*
Slow curtain as light fades.)

IT SHOULD HAPPEN TO A DOG

AUTHOR'S NOTE

It Should Happen to a Dog is a serio-comic strip, which, those who know the story of Jonah will see, is faithful to the original. If the characters speak as people we know personally, it is because there is no other way for us to know characters. If Jonah is somewhat familiar in his manner of address to the Almighty – it is because one may assume that a greater intimacy exists between prophets and their source of instruction than does for the rest of us.

In the staging of *It Should Happen to a Dog,* a coat-stand is required from which the rope of the ship is hung, and upon which any practical props may also hang. The coat-stand becomes the tree in the last scene, and should be placed behind Jonah's back in full view of the audience by the Angel or by a property man who may be written in at the director's discretion. A thunder-sheet will be found useful. The characters should be dressed in an anachronistic selection of garments suggestive of our own time and of biblical times, and the piece should be played at a fast tempo.

As to the message of the story – 'Why should I not spare Nineveh?' This is, one hopes, how God feels about Man – unlike Man who is less tolerant of himself.

Characters

JONAH

MAN / SAILOR / KING / ANGEL

It Should Happen to a Dog was first produced for television and was broadcast in 1955 by the BBC, with the following company:

JONAH, Alfie Bass
MAN, David Kossof

Directed by Tony Richardson

It Should Happen to a Dog

SCENE ONE

JONAH: Please, please, what do you want from my life? He
won't leave me alone. All these years I've been running
– a traveller – Jonah, the traveller, representing Top Hat;
Braces For The Trousers; Fair Lady Fancy Buttons; Hold
Tight Hair Grips – only good brands in the suitcase. Ask
them in Tarshish, ask them in Aleppo, in Carthage even;
they all know Jonah ben Amittai, regular call once a month
for more than thirty years. I don't complain, only I'm
tired of running, that's all. Now at last I'm tired. I get this
good pitch here – at last – so I shouldn't have to run with a
suitcase any more. And still he nags me. All right. I heard.
I'm going. What happens to me shouldn't happen to a dog.
(*A MAN stands in his way.*)

MAN: It's a nice pitch you got here.

JONAH: It's nice.

MAN: So what are you looking so down in the mouth for?

JONAH: What's the use of talking? It has to happen to me.

MAN: What happens?

JONAH: This dream.

MAN: Dream?

JONAH: I tell you, this is a most terrible dream. The voice
comes like the voice of a bird. In the middle hours of the
night it comes chirping, chirping, 'The end of the world is
at hand. The end of the world is at hand.'

MAN: Could be right. It wouldn't be the first time.

JONAH: So all right then, let it be the end of the world. Is it
my business? Am I to blame?

MAN: And this is *all* the voice says?

JONAH: (*Lying.*) Certainly that's all. Isn't it enough? What else
should it say?

MAN: Nothing. Only if that is all the voice says you got
nothing to worry about. Look – if it *is* the end of the world,
what can you do? On the other hand – if it isn' t – you got

nothing to worry about. I'll take a quarter ounce Archangel
Gabriel tobacco.

JONAH: (*Handing him a small packet of tobacco.*) That's a good
brand. I opened up the Tarshish territory for Archangel
Gabriel.

MAN: I never smoke nothing else. (*Starts to go out.*)

JONAH: Aye, aye.

MAN: Oh. (*Giving coin.*) Chirp, chirp? Chirp, chirp, heh, heh.
(*As he goes.*)

JONAH: I hate birds. You know what it says? 'Arise, Jonah,
arise. Go to Nineveh, that great city, and cry against it.' I
ask you. Why pick on me? Why sort me out? Chirp, chirp.
It's in my head the whole time. Once I could sleep fifteen
hours – like a short course of death. No more. I don't sleep
that good no more. I hate birds. (*To God.*) All right, I'm
going – to the docks – for a ship – I'm going.
(*He walks into the next area and set-up.*)

SCENE TWO

(*The same MAN as before, as a SAILOR, is untying a rope from
a capstan as JONAH enters.*)

JONAH: (*To God.*) Certainly I'm on my way. By ship. You
expect me to fly? If you are so clever and in such a hurry,
make me sprout a couple of wings so I'll take off. It's
quicker by air. But so far is only invented the ship. (*To the
SAILOR.*) Which way you going, shipmate?

SAILOR: Tarshish.

JONAH: You don't say. I got a lot of friends there. It's a
beautiful place. In Tarshish they got more people over a
hundred years old than anywhere else.

SAILOR: Who wants to live so long?

JONAH: In some circumstances, chirp, chirp, who gets a
chance to live so long? Tarshish, eh? (*Aside.*) It seems silly,
if I'm going all this way to Nineveh – where I am certainly
eventually going – why don't I break my journey and look
up a few old friends in Tarshish. Why not? (*To the SAILOR.*)
It's a crime? You can take passengers?

SAILOR: First class or tourist?

JONAH: In the old days when I was travelling for myself, nothing but first class for J B Amittai. But in these circumstances, one tourist.

SAILOR: Single or return?

JONAH: What's the matter with you? Return, of course. I got a wonderful little business waiting for me when I come back.

SAILOR: (*Shouts.*) One more tourist coming up. Tarshish return.

JONAH: (*Aside, as he begins to board ship.*) I'll spend a couple of days there to build my strength up and then I'll give such a shout against Nineveh. After all, it's a tough territory, and what difference can a couple of days make? Thank you. (*Sits.*) Oh, it's a beautiful day for sailing. Any more for the Skylark?
(*Blackout.*)

SCENE THREE

(*JONAH asleep on some bales of goods. The SAILOR wakes him.*)

JONAH: Chirp, chirp. The end of the world is at hand. (*He wakes up.*)

SAILOR: If it isn't troubling you.

JONAH: The weather's come over black all of a sudden.

SAILOR: In all my years I never knew a storm this time of the year.

JONAH: Are we far from Tarshish?

SAILOR: Are you barmy ? We been stuck out here the past five hours, and all the wind does is try to blow us back. In all my years I never see anything like it.

JONAH: Very interesting phenomena. Like St Ermin's fire; caused by electricity in the atmosphere, you understand? And take the sea serpent, for example.

SAILOR: I will.

JONAH: The sea serpent is really a very big eel. Science proves it.

SAILOR: I don't take any chances. After I tried every trick I know, I pray. (*He prays for a few moments. Then he looks at JONAH.*) You too, guv'ner.

JONAH: I already said my prayers today. To duplicate is just silly. When it comes to the evening I'll say my evening prayers.

SAILOR: Don't take no chances. Pray now.

JONAH: It should happen to a dog what happens to me. Listen, God. Stop messing me about. Didn't I give you my word of honour I will go to Nineveh? Ask anybody anywhere in these territories. Jonah's word is his bond. (*A gale begins to blow.*) Do me a favour just this once. I will catch the first boat from Tarshish to Nineveh. The very first boat. (*The gale blows stronger.*)

SAILOR: Did you make a sacrifice yet? We got all the passengers making sacrifices to all the different gods. That way we must hit the right god sooner or later and he'll stop the storm. Guv'ner, did you make a sacrifice yet?

JONAH: Here. I sacrifice this beautiful meat pie. I only ate a small portion of it.

SAILOR: Right. Throw it overboard with an appropriate prayer.

JONAH: Here, God. And remember I'm catching the first boat from Tarshish. All right? (*He throws the pie overboard. The pie is thrown straight back, and JONAH catches it. The SAILOR looks at him significantly, then calls out.*)

SAILOR: Aye, aye. This is it folks.

JONAH: It's a perfectly natural phenomena.

SAILOR: This man is the trouble-maker.

JONAH: It's got a perfectly natural explanation.

SAILOR: His sacrifice was definitely refused. He's the one. Overboard with him – overboard. (*He advances on JONAH.*)

JONAH: You can't do this to me. I am on very important business. I can drown in there. What happens to me should happen to a dog. (*He backs away from the influence of the SAILOR till he falls overboard. The gale stops and the sun comes out.*)

SAILOR: I never did like the look of that fella. To me, he always looked a trouble-maker. Uh? What? (*He follows the*

progress of JONAH in the water.) You could live a thousand years, you wouldn't see a man swallowed by a whale. But who would believe such a story.
(*Blackout.*)

SCENE FOUR

(*JONAH gropes in the dark, then strikes a match.*)
JONAH: Faugh – it smells like Billingsgate in here. All right. Now what am I supposed to do. Now I can't go to Nineveh. All I wanted to do was to go to Nineveh and cry against it, and look at me. Maybe I'm dead. I must be dead. Who would have thought that being dead was a black-out in a fish shop? Maybe *this is* the end of the world. But if it isn't, if, for example, don't laugh, I happen to have been swallowed by a whale, tee-hee, I categorically put it on record that if I could go to Nineveh at this moment I would definitely and unconditionally go to Nineveh at this moment.
(*A crash of thunder; lightning. JONAH executes a double somersault into the light. Looks round, amazed.*)
Honestly, God, sometimes I can't make you out. You've got such a mysterious way of carrying on. (*He stretches himself.*) So where's Tarshish? Tarshish. (*Disgusted.*) If I'm not dead and if I'm not mistaken and if my memory serves me right that great city in the distance is – *Nineveh.* It should happen to a dog. (*Exit, towards Nineveh.*)

SCENE FIVE

KING: (*Enters, sits, sorts papers, looks up.*) Jonah B Amittai.
JONAH: Yes, Your Majesty.
KING: You are up on a charge of vagrancy.
JONAH: Uh?
KING: Vagrancy.
JONAH: Oh.
KING: Also it seems you have been talking a lot of seditious nonsense about the end of the world is at hand. Also – what' s this? Also you keep saying 'chirp, chirp'. This

official work is beginning to get me down. All night long I get the most terrible dreams. Mmm – what have you got to say for yourself?

JONAH: Just a minute. (*He mounts the throne and sings.*) The Lord saith: Cry out against Nineveh, that great city, for their wickedness is come up before me. Stop. Yet forty days and Nineveh shall be overthrown. Stop. The end of the world is at hand. Stop. Repent lest ye perish. End of message. And that, Your Majesty, in short, is what I am instructed to tell you. (*Sits.*) Personally it makes no difference to me. I should be just as pleased for Nineveh not to be destroyed. For my part it can go on being as wicked as you like, though, if you was to ask my opinion, as a businessman of some experience, I'll tell you straight out that honesty is always the best policy. A satisfied client is better than Government consuls. Especially as, I am instructed to tell you, the Government is not going to last too long, anyway.

KING: What's the source of your information?

JONAH: A little bird tells me every night.

KING: (*Alarmed.*) A bird?

JONAH: A little bird. Chirp, chirp. It makes just like that.

KING: What colour the feathers?

JONAH: The feathers! One wing is blue, the other wing white, the breast red, the tail purple, but the funny thing is, this bird has one brown eye and…

KING: …and the other a blue!

JONAH: You are familiar with it?

KING: I have been getting the same dream.

JONAH: Oh. So *your* little bird tells *me* one hundred times nightly to come to Nineveh and inform *you* that in forty days from now *you* are completely in liquidation. And that's what *I'm* telling *you*? It's a madhouse here!

KING: (*Stands up and tears his robe.*) Let neither man nor beast, herd nor flock, taste anything. Let them not eat food nor drink water; but let man and beast be covered with sackcloth and cry mightily unto God. Yea, let them turn everyone from his evil way, and from the violence that is in their hands. Let them turn from the violence that is in their hands for the sake of the smallest bird, for the bird also is God. (*To JONAH.*) Who can tell if God will turn and repent, and turn away from his fierce anger, that we perish not?

JONAH: Who can tell? But if you ask my opinion, I don't think so. Otherwise he doesn't go to all this trouble. No, King, this is the end. Still, you can always try. There's no charge for trying.

(*Exeunt.*)

SCENE SIX

(*JONAH is sitting on a rock in the scorching sun. In the background a celebratory fairground noise, like a bank holiday Monday.*)

JONAH: It should happen to a dog, what happens to me. Here after all this the King himself takes my personal word that in forty days it is the end of the world; and what happens? The forty-first day is proclaimed a national holiday. Government stock rises, and I am the biggest bloody fool in the Middle East. I am a laughing stock, that's all, a laughing stock. I don't move. I'm going to sit here until I get a sun stroke. You can do what you like with Nineveh, miniver, shminever. I'm finished. 'Yet forty days and Nineveh shall be overthrown.'

(*Laughter off and voices singing: 'Jonah, Jonah – he pulled a boner'.*)

Listen to 'em. Laugh your heads off! Three, four hours I won't hear you any more. And I won't hear that damned bird either no more. I hate birds. (*A shadow is thrown over JONAH.*) What's this? By my life. A tree!

(*A palm tree has sprung up from nowhere. He reaches down a coconut.*)

What do you know? Coconuts as well with a patent zipper. You just pull it open and drink the milk. Ice-cold. Delicious. And what's this. The *Tarshish Gazette*. Well, this is certainly a novelty. (*Reads.*) Aha. I see that Mrs Zinkin has been presented with her third daughter. That's bad.

Young Fyvel is opening a café-espresso bar on the High
Street. That's a good position. He should do well. It's just
like a summer holiday here now, and believe me, I earned
a vacation. This is certainly a wonderful place you made
here, Lord. I got to hand it to you. For land development
you're the tops.

(*Standing beside him is the MAN dressed as an ANGEL. JONAH
sees him and looks away, back to his paper.*)

ANGEL: A beautiful day.

JONAH: Yes, it's certainly marvellous weather we're having.

ANGEL: That's a remarkable palm tree. (*He reaches out for a
coconut.*) This I never saw before –

JONAH: It's got a zipper.

ANGEL: What will he think of next, eh?

(*He offers the coconut to the irritable JONAH.*)

JONAH: (*Throwing down the newspaper.*) All right. Cut out the
performance. You are an angel, right?

ANGEL: I must give you credit, Jonah. You're certainly quick
off the mark.

JONAH: But an angel?

ANGEL: Archangel.

JONAH: Oh – so now what do I have to do? Go back to
Nineveh? Tell the King the Lord has changed his mind
again? He is going to give him ten more days and then
bring the world to an end? He made a laughing stock of
me.

ANGEL: What can you do?

JONAH: Admitted. But at the same time this is a terrible way
to treat someone who goes through all the trouble I go
through. For what – only He knows. And He won't tell.
(*Turns, bangs into tree.*) Feh! Fancy trees yet!

ANGEL: (*Wheedling.*) That's certainly a *wonderful* tree. Help
yourself.

JONAH: Perhaps just another coconut. These coconuts are
delicious.

(*As he turns, the tree withers, collapsing into dust; that is, the
coat-stand is removed.*)

What a terrible thing to happen. Such a wonderful tree. With such trees mankind could live in plenty for ever. A quick death from some palm tree disease, I suppose?

ANGEL: It's a small worm crawls through the arterial system of the tree, cuts off the life from the heart. And boom.

JONAH: A quick death to that worm.

ANGEL: Ah. You notice something. How annoyed you are with this worm which after all only killed a tree, which after all didn't cause you an hour's work. After all, you don't hear God complain; He made the tree to come up in a night. He can make it go down the night after.

JONAH: It cranks me such a beautiful tree should die like that, apart from now I am in the sun again and can catch a sun stroke any minute. Pity about the tree. Hey-hey. This is some kind of parable, ain't it? You are trying to teach me something, isn't it?

ANGEL: That's my boy. By this little experiment He is saying, if you feel sorry for the tree, which after all didn't cost you anything, why shouldn't He feel sorry for Nineveh, that great city, in which there are one hundred and twenty thousand human beings on whom after all He has taken a great deal of trouble even if they still don't know what time it is, or their left hand from their right hand. Also much cattle.

JONAH: You got a point there, there was never any harm in those cattle. But if you don't mind a question…

ANGEL: Any help I can give you.

JONAH: If God knew right from the start exactly what He is going to do about everything – right?

ANGEL: That's right.

JONAH: Then He knows He isn't going to destroy Nineveh. Right?

ANGEL: Right!

JONAH: Then what does He want of my life? What's the point of all this expensive business with whales and palm trees and so on?

ANGEL: You mankind, you can't see no further than your nose.

JONAH: So what's the answer?

ANGEL: You see – (*Long pause.*) frankly, I don't know.

JONAH: It should happen to a dog.

ANGEL: Me too. After all, it's no joke following you or any other prophet I happen to get assigned to around the whole time. You think it's such a wonderful thing to be an angel and do a few conjuring tricks? It *should* happen to a dog.

JONAH: On the other hand, come to think of it, whose dogs are we?

ANGEL: We are the dogs of God.

JONAH So...

ANGEL: Nu?

JONAH: Whatever happens to a dog...

ANGEL: ...must happen to us, eh? (*He chuckles with admiration.*)

JONAH: Can you give me a lift back home?

ANGEL: It's a pleasure.

(*JONAH jumps on ANGEL's back.*)

JONAH: On the way we could call in at Tarshish. I got a lot of friends there.

ANGEL: That's a good idea. So have I. (*As they go out.*) Did you hear that young Fyvel opened a café-espresso bar on the High Street?

JONAH: I read it in the paper. He's a clever boy.

(*Curtain.*)

THE MIGHTY HUNTER

AUTHOR'S NOTE

The Mighty Hunter draws upon both biblical and folk sources to tell the familiar moral story of the successful man who forgets that he remains a man.

In Nimrod himself there is no more harm than you might reasonably expect to find in a man. There is also no more good. At opening Nimrod is a man with problems which we would be glad for him to solve, wishing as we always do to see harm reduced and good multiplied. Successive scenes enact Nimrod's sense of harm growing while good correspondingly diminishes. There is, therefore, in the character of Nimrod, progress – for he gets steadily worse.

In the old man there is no progress. He is what he always was – an old Adam trying in vain to shed the burden which the power to succeed always becomes to a man. Because he is a failure himself he finds malicious satisfaction in his knowledge that, from Napoleon to Nimrod, men have not been able to succeed without humility and decency giving way to destructive omnipotence.

And because Adam believes that only God is Power safely, the powerful man being no more than an amateur thief in a short night, he takes Nimrod's fall to be yet another proof that all power is for the worst in the most powerless of all possible worlds.

The old man should accompany his little songs (which may be set to any convenient tune), with little dances of a suitable nature.

Nimrod should be played as an American or European in the prime of life which continues until the truth strikes home to him and he returns from Babel speaking back-slang. Then he should age rapidly.

In staging, tempo and continuity should be played for, the stage, where possible, being already set up in areas which simply represent Nimrod's successive situations. Or, alternatively, the piece can be played in two acting areas against blacks. On the cross-fade and covered by the old man's songs and dances, scene-changes could then be made in the Nimrod area.

Characters

NIMROD

MAN with a long white beard

The Mighty Hunter was first performed on 25 July 1956 at the New Lindsey Theatre, London.

The Mighty Hunter

SCENE ONE

(*A MAN with a long white beard, carrying a brown paper parcel, is revealed at the mouth of a desert tent. He sings:*)

MAN: When Adam delved and Eve span
At least there was no argument
About which one was the man.

A man is a man and it ain't very much
Even a King is more or less
The same kind of miserable crawling thing.

Is anybody at home?

NIMROD: (*From within.*) No.

MAN: You quite certain?

NIMROD: Absolutely positive.

MAN: (*Bitterly.*) Desert hospitality. Come in – make yourself comfortable – have a few dates – let me wash your feet. In a pig's eye. (*He spits, starts to go out and calls back.*) Don't think I'm being rude, but may a triple curse alight on your shoulders and from there proceed to blight your organs of sight, taste, and especially generation.

(*NIMROD emerges from the tent.*)

NIMROD: Would you please mind repeating those few remarks?

MAN: I'd be glad to.

NIMROD: Look, old man, in the ordinary way I am the most hospitable of desert Arabs. In fact Nimrod is known in the black tents everywhere as a very good fellow. It's just that –

MAN: I know, I know. 'It's just that – ' with everybody. You treat your fellow man like a brother when you happen to be feeling brotherly. Which doesn't happen to be today. I perfectly understand, and as I said before, may a triple curse –

NIMROD: May I point out that my flocks have been stolen, my men have deserted me, my three wives have run away with three of the ugliest goatherds you ever saw in your

163

WOLF MANKOWITZ: THE PLAYS

life? I have a few dried figs left, that's all, and a jar of water, but if that's your idea of comfort, for my part come in and make yourself comfortable.

MAN: I accept your kind invitation. So you're Nimrod, eh?

NIMROD: For my sins –

MAN: It's a just reward. I have to admit that the sight of you cheers me up considerably, because I personally am a bankrupt of long standing, but if the same thing can happen to a famous man like you, it makes me feel a little better.

NIMROD: Have a fig.

(*The MAN takes a fig and begins to chew it.*)

MAN: It's a fair quality fig.

NIMROD: To think, when I was born the fortune-teller predicted a big future for me. The lousy old crone was lying.

MAN: You could still have big things ahead of you.

NIMROD: Big things – they left me one camel, and – I never saw it happen before – that died from drinking too much water.

MAN: Constriction of the hump.

NIMROD: My future is a thing of the past.

(*The MAN finishes the fig, drinks water from the flask, dusts himself down, and stands up.*)

MAN: Look Nimrod, I'm not going to beat about the bush. I have here something which is just your line of country.

NIMROD: A salesman. The only people who ever call on me nowadays want to sell sheep-dip and I've got no sheep, or date-palm spray and the palms have long since withered away. Draw your own conclusion – I don't have any money.

MAN: Who's talking about money? Look at this. (*He unwraps the parcel and takes from it a flashily cut hunting jacket and trousers.*) I have here the finest two-piece hunting suit you ever saw in your life. Go in the tent and try it on.

NIMROD: How shall I pay?

MAN: Don't worry about paying. Try on the suit.

(*NIMROD goes into the tent.*)

You'll find it's a perfect fit. Trousers not too tight?

NIMROD: They're like custom-made for me.

MAN: I was a bit worried about the trousers. I want to tell you, Nimrod, that this very suit was the one worn by Adam when he was thrown out of Eden – you know the old story?

NIMROD: You don't say –

MAN: I do say. If you don't believe me look at the label inside the jacket.

NIMROD: (*Looking out of tent.*) This is a great honour even if it is a second-hand suit.

MAN: It isn't only a great honour, it's a definite business advantage. This suit has magical powers, and in your situation nothing short of magic is going to make any difference.

(*NIMROD comes out dressed very smartly in the hunting jacket and trousers.*)

Ah-hah – already you begin to look like something. A well-dressed man inspires confidence. It doesn't matter where you go, what you do, appearances count.

NIMROD: It's my style all right. What kind of magic do you have in mind?

MAN: (*Intimately.*) Wearing this suit whatever you hunt you can catch.

NIMROD: (*Sceptical.*) I see. Just a minute, I'll give you back the suit.

MAN: What's the matter? You don't like to catch what you hunt?

NIMROD: You think I was born yesterday? This is the oldest confidence trick in the world.

MAN: So what do you lose if it's a confidence trick? Isn't confidence exactly what you need? Quick, get your bow and arrow. I can feel there's a flight of geese coming over. Quick.

(*NIMROD seizes his bow and arrow and fires into the air. A ready-cooked goose, wrapped in a serviette, falls down onto the stage with the arrow through it. NIMROD picks up the goose.*)

Isn't that service?

(*NIMROD tears a leg off the goose and is about to devour it.*)
Manners. I am your guest.
(*He takes the leg from NIMROD and delicately chews it.*)
Delicious. Try the other leg.)

NIMROD: (*As they eat.*) It's a wonderful suit, but how can I afford such luxuries? I already told you how I'm fixed.

MAN: The suit is yours for nothing.

NIMROD: For nothing?

MAN: For practically nothing.

NIMROD: That's what I thought. I'll give you back the suit.

MAN: Nimrod, I know just how you feel – look, my hunting days are over – I'm going to let you have the suit –

NIMROD: But I'm telling you. I'm not worth practically nothing. I'm worth nothing, and that's the sum total both gross and net.

MAN: Keep the suit – so long as you remember you are not even practically nothing, that you are less than nothing. Keep the suit so long as you remember – you are only a man.

NIMROD: Aren't I the first to admit it?

(*They shake hands and as NIMROD moves into the next set-up now in darkness, the MAN comes forward and sings:*)

MAN: You human chaps who want to be successful
    Try still to stay as human as you can
    Yet what's the fun in being so successful
    If you remain an ordinary man?

SCENE TWO

(*NIMROD, now a hunter-baron, is revealed surrounded by stuffed animals and birds. He calls offstage.*)

NIMROD: Give those twenty-seven giant Irish deer I just shot to the poor. (*To audience.*) I just can't stand the sight of meat. Even a little *fillet mignon* in a delicate sauce turns my stomach. I suppose it's the price I have to pay for being such a mighty hunter.

(*The MAN now walks into NIMROD's area.*)

MAN: Well, Nimrod, in the past few years you have certainly become a mighty hunter.

NIMROD: Do you have an appointment?

MAN: May a curse alight on your shoulders and thrice blight –

NIMROD: Oh, it's you, my old friend.

MAN: What's the matter? All of a sudden you're such an important man people got to have an appointment with you?

NIMROD: So many people calling the whole time – shoot this, shoot that – my life wouldn't be my own if I didn't make myself a little hard to get. But to you, my benefactor, I am always at home. Have a little vegetable salad with a couple of nut cutlets. Very tasty – I suppose. (*He toys with his salad.*)

MAN: Thank you – no. So how does it feel to be famous? You're quite a celebrity. I heard the other day you killed an unusually large three-headed dragon in Joppa.

NIMROD: That three-headed dragon was over-estimated. Two of his heads he hadn't even any teeth in.

MAN: Never mind. It was a good work.

NIMROD: Before, when it was difficult to hunt something and dangerous to fight it, I used to enjoy the game. Today – to be the mightiest hunter in the world, my friend, is still to be nothing.

MAN: Nimrod – I think you're going to work out all right. How are your wives?

NIMROD: I'm only on speaking terms with seventeen of them.

MAN: That's still too much talk. And your flocks? I bet they've multiplied beyond words.

NIMROD: I don't even know what the latest stock figure is.

MAN: And your retainers? Like an army, I bet. Battalions of them, complete with banners.

NIMROD: The damn fools talk about nothing except hunting, fishing and shooting.

MAN: Still, you are certainly a mighty hunter.

NIMROD: That's nothing.

MAN: Quite right. And now I'll tell you something. This suit of yours, Nimrod, can make you the principal chieftain in this area.

NIMROD: That could be interesting.

MAN: Interesting – you could be a blessing to the whole territory. You could unite all the tribes around here into one big happy family. Prosperity would reign, and so, incidentally, would you.

NIMROD: Maybe I could found a dynasty based on fair dealing, good faith, friendly relations and all the rest of that stuff.

MAN: If you put your mind to it, Nimrod, I think you could.

NIMROD: I'll do it.

MAN: Live for ever, King Nimrod. Isn't that the expression? Live for ever – heh, heh.

(*As NIMROD walks off into the next set-up, now dark, the MAN dances forward and sings:*)

> I always like to meet a fellow
> Keeps his mind on higher things.
> But when he starts to talk too mellow
> Brother, I quick count my rings.

SCENE THREE

(*NIMROD, now a king, revealed in a hall filled with banners, cutlasses, suits of armour and other warlike devices.*)

NIMROD: (*Calls off.*) Tell the last nineteen hundred and fifty-five complainants to come again tomorrow. I settled enough disputes for one day. Being a king is a pretty full-time job.

(*The MAN enters.*)

MAN: King Nimrod, live for ever. (*He giggles.*)

NIMROD: And what makes you think I want to live for ever? I am seeing no more complainants today.

MAN: May a triple curse alight on your shoulders –

NIMROD: It's you again? I'm glad you called in.

MAN: King of Upper and Lower. That's something it's worthwhile to be.

NIMROD: Founding a dynasty based on fair dealing, good faith, and friendly relations is all right.

MAN: I should say so.

NIMROD: Except you have to deal with a lot of crooked dealers, bad faith, and you have no friends.

MAN: How are your wives?

168

NIMROD: The Association of Kings have an established
rule – you never ask them this question.

MAN: At least your army is a highly disciplined organisation.

NIMROD: The army is so highly trained I have to lay on
ceremonial parades every day to stop them revolting out of
sheer restlessness. I get a creak in my arm from saluting.

MAN: The suit goes very well with the crown. It must be a
wonderful feeling to achieve prosperity for one's people
and all that stuff.

NIMROD: It's all right – but now we are so prosperous all
the kings around are jealous. They want to be cut in on
a percentage. I am spending night after night with the
diplomatic corps down at the Foreign Office. It's a terrible
headache. You always told me: remember I am only a
man.

MAN: That's right.

NIMROD: Correction. I am only a man with a headache.

MAN: I didn't want to tell you before, Nimrod, but this suit
you're wearing –

NIMROD: Here it comes.

MAN: By this suit you could peaceably conquer all the nations
of the world. Not, you understand me, in any spirit of
aggression, but for the highest of motives. Firstly to defend
the prosperity of your people; secondly to institute fair
dealing, good faith and friendly relations everywhere.

NIMROD: You mean peace in our time?

MAN: That's a good phrase for it.

NIMROD: This would be something for a man to do. This is
worth doing.

MAN: Everybody has always thought so, and, I think I can say
that, without doubt, I personally agree with them in this
matter.

NIMROD: Peaceable unification. That's the thing.

MAN: Two good phrases in one day – this is something to
remember.

(*NIMROD walks off as before. The MAN dances forward and
sings:*)

SCENE FOUR

MAN: If I fight my brother man
    It's purely out of brotherhood,
    For every blow I ever struck
    Struck down the bad to make 'em good.

    If you will not be my brother
    I will hit you on the head –
    For if you don't know how to love me
    You, my friend, are happier dead.

That Nimrod is certainly taking his time subduing the Malachites. Of course, the Malachites have a secret weapon – the horse. But I have a feeling Nimrod will win. (*NIMROD enters with a sword, crying off.*)

NIMROD: Raze the city to the ground, plant it with salt, kill off the women and children, and paste up a notice declaring universal brotherhood.

MAN: That was a nice gesture, Nimrod. The women and children, if they were still alive, would really appreciate that.

NIMROD: I'm going to get myself some of those horses the Malachites were using. Personally I think the horse has a great future, especially in cavalry warfare.

MAN: It's a noble animal, all right.

NIMROD: It certainly is. Are you a Malachite? Because if so, I'm afraid I shall have to cut you to pieces.

MAN: May a thrice curse alight on your shoulders, making your sword into a lightning conductor so you get burnt to death the next time there's a storm, which should be quite soon.

NIMROD: I didn't recognize you. You know – the heat of battle. They put up a great fight, but right triumphed in the end.

MAN: That goes without saying. Who's next on your list for peaceable unification?

NIMROD: I'll have a look. (*He gets out a list.*) Would you believe it? There's no one left. This is a moment of great feeling for me. I have, after all these years, unified the world.

MAN: I suppose you could quite reasonably call yourself the Emperor?

NIMROD: If you insist. I think that's justifiable in the circumstances. 'Emperor Nimrod'.

MAN: It's quite usual. So what now?

NIMROD: The three R-s. Reorganization, Relief funds, Reconstruction. Everything will be better than before.

MAN: I can see it all. You'll build blocks of flats, with hot and cold running water, and kindergartens for the ruined children from ruined homes. You have done well – with the suit, Nimrod.

NIMROD: (*Pensively.*) When I finish my rebuilding programme – what will I do?

MAN: It's bound to take a long time. With luck, by the time you finish, you'll be dead.

NIMROD: That's true. (*Alarmed.*) That's true. Here my life is passing away in the public service, and at the end of it – nothing but death?

MAN: This is what I am always saying to you. You are only a man, and consequently, at the end, you have to die.

NIMROD: But is it right? Is it fair? Look at everything I've done. Do ordinary men do all this?

MAN: (*Aside.*) Only if they are properly dressed for the job. It's all in the suit.

NIMROD: And if every man can't do all this, and I do, doesn't it make me something out of the ordinary?

MAN: (*Aside.*) Only if you happen to have the suit, you follow – take no notice otherwise – the moral is coming.

NIMROD: In which case, why should I die? There should be some special dispensation, some special arrangement – something.

MAN: I got a feeling you're barking up the wrong tree, Nimrod. You get on building the kindergartens. Don't worry about these other things. You're a good boy – but brains is never your strong suit.

NIMROD: I must build, build higher. (*Exiting.*) Build, build.

MAN: That's the right spirit. You build. I hope success didn't go to his head.

(*The MAN dances forward and sings:*)

Now all you boys who make success
Jump on your knees like a laughing baby.
Remember please the end must come
Without a doubt, or an if, or a maybe.

Whatever you do,
At the end, my friend,
You are only a man
Without a plan. (*Exit.*)

SCENE FIVE

(*NIMROD is revealed against scaffolding and building materials hurriedly working over contracts and tenders.*)

NIMROD: (*Calls off.*) Make that two million more stock bricks. Requisition scaffolding everywhere. Send three thousand political malcontents up from the salt mine and put them on digging foundations.

(*The MAN enters carrying another parcel.*)

MAN: Such an activity – this is certainly the greatest reconstruction programme in history.

NIMROD: That last shipment of cement was inferior quality. I am going to have your nose and ears cut off, and please don't do it again.

MAN: Do I have to curse you? What a terrible memory for faces.

NIMROD: It's you again – I'm sorry – you look exactly like a cement contractor.

MAN: His beard is white only from the cement. This is the genuine article. I got to give you credit, Nimrod, you're certainly a mighty builder. But how come people are still living in filthy hovels, children playing in the gutter, the temples falling to pieces, and not a single public library in the whole city?

NIMROD: We are too busy building just now. These other things will all come in time. Just now we have a very big

172

defence project on hand. (*He calls up.*) Send those slaves back to the salt mines and get fresh ones to work on the hanging gardens. The tower has to look attractive. After all, when it's finished I'm having a meeting with God on top of it – appearances are important when you're going to negotiate a pact – put on all the bullshit you can muster.

MAN: I beg your pardon?

NIMROD: We're building a tower here so high it will touch Heaven.

MAN: And then?

NIMROD: Then with due ceremony I'll climb the tower. On top of it there's a properly constructed cedar-wood and sheet-gold council chamber.

MAN: The latest style – no expense spared.

NIMROD: And in the council chamber God and I with our appropriate dignitaries to blot the agreements and bring glasses of water – we'll talk over the whole question.

MAN: What question?

NIMROD: (*Irritably.*) This whole business of everybody dying the whole time. This is my thesis – I am prepared to admit that it's right and proper for ordinary men to die. But for me, after all the work I've done for the public service – it's a scandal. Don't tell me to pray – the priests haven't the slightest contact with God on this question. I just have to negotiate it myself, that's all. In the end I have to do everything myself.

MAN: Am I quite clear on this? You mean to tell me you are going to make a deal with God?

NIMROD: The least He can do is discuss the question with me, not behave in this high-handed way. After all, look at the sacrifices I made – seven hundred thousand Lemonites, five hundred thousand Hezekites. Who bids so high as me? And if He won't come to terms I'll just have to give Him a serious talking-to, that's all. (*He shouts off.*) Put up more scaffolding there. It's like the leaning tower of Pisa. It's already so high it takes a year for a single brick to get to the top. Even at the lowest level you have to admit that's certainly some tower, isn't it?

MAN: (*Bitterly depressed.*) It always happens like this. No matter how good it looks at the start, in the end this always has to happen.

NIMROD: (*Shouting off.*) Get on with it there, you cretinous peasants. Do I have to do everything myself? (*Exit.*)

MAN: I'll just have to take the suit back again, that's all. Don't think I'm getting above myself, Lord, but this is becoming too much of a routine. The same thing happened with Alexander. With Julius Caesar exactly the same thing. With Napoleon. They borrow the suit from old Adam – that's me for those who didn't already realise it – and in no time they want to talk special terms with God. I always carry a sheet of brown paper and a piece of string – the suit always comes back. (*He gets out brown paper and string.*) What are you going to do, Lord? Strike him dead?

(*Enter NIMROD, confused.*)

NIMROD: I-ay ont-day owe-nay ot-way ee-thay ell-hay as-hay um-kay ove-ray em-thay all-hay.

MAN: I beg your pardon.

NIMROD: Ay-thay ont-day alk-tay English-ay. (*A babel off.*)

MAN: Everybody's talking different languages.

(*As he talks, the MAN takes the jacket and trousers off the confused NIMROD, who is left standing in the clothes he wore when the story began.*)

Now this is a very interesting experience – unique even in my lifetime. What were you calling the tower?

NIMROD: Abel-bay.

(*The MAN wraps up the jacket and trousers in the brown paper, making a parcel.*)

MAN: Abel-bay? You mean Babel. Who would have thought of that? Lord, you are strictly in a class on your own.

NIMROD: Oo-day umthing-say.

(*The MAN picks up the other parcel.*)

MAN: I have just the thing for you.

(*NIMROD undoes the parcel rapidly. It contains a series of books entitled 'How to Learn Italian', Greek, French, German, etc.*)

NIMROD: Owe-say ot-way oo-day I-ay oo-day?

MAN: Nimrod, I hope you're a good linguist. Only, sonny, take a tip from me – I been all over – always get your fundamental grammar right. Now I suppose I got to find some other sucker who will take the suit.
(*He makes to go out, then turns to watch NIMROD looking at the books.*)

NIMROD: (*Slowly and painfully learning the truth.*) Emember-ray oo-yay ar-yay ownly-ay a-yay an-may – Re-mem-ber – you – are – on-ly – a – man. (*Repeated with growing, desperate awareness as the curtain falls, leaving the MAN front of curtain.*)

MAN: (*To the audience.*) You also. Remember. (*Exit, singing:*)

> A man is a man and it ain't very much,
> Even a king is more or less
> The same kind of miserable, crawling thing.